Managing the Bull

Detect and Deflect the Crap

A No-Nonsense Approach to Personal Finance

David Christianson, BA, R.F.P., CFP, TEP

KNOWLEDGE BUREAU
NEWSBOOKS

WINNIPEG, MANITOBA, CANADA

David Christianson

MANAGING THE BULL
Detect and deflect the crap

Printed and bound in Canada

Cataloguing data available from Library and Archives Canada

Christianson, David, 1956 -
    Managing the Bull: Detect and Deflect the Crap

Published by:
Knowledge Bureau, Inc.
187 St. Mary's Road, Winnipeg, Manitoba Canada R2H 1J2
204-953-4769
Email: reception@knowledgebureau.com

Publisher: Evelyn Jacks
Editor: Suzanne Wray
Cover Design and Layout: Think Shift Advertising Inc.
Page Design and Layout: Typeworks

Acknowledgements

This is for Vera, who has been with me the whole journey, and my great kids Sarah and Taylor.

Thanks to Sheril Kowerko and Craig Kepron, who have run the business so I could expand my educational offerings, and to Hugh Latimer, my mentor in so many things.

Special thanks to Evelyn Jacks, who has pulled me through obstacles so many times and convinced me to publish my collected wisdom, and to Suzanne Wray and David Roberts, great editors and writers, without whom this book would never have been completed.

I am blessed with many other incredible people in my life who provide me tremendous support, encouragement and unconditional positive regard in all aspects of my life, like sailing, music, running and, occasionally, partying.

You know who you are....thanks!

And most of all, to our fabulous clients, who have worked with us, trusted us and taught us so much.

David Christianson
July, 2012

Table of Contents

Preface

THIS BOOK IS REALLY ABOUT happiness and success. Yours.

That may seem an odd statement in a book about money, and it's not made because we think money can buy happiness.

Happiness comes from being grateful for what you have. So, happiness is really a state of mind, and it can be achieved at any time.

Almost all people are happiest when they feel that their personal and financial situation is improving, and they have a hopeful and optimistic outlook on the future. Setting goals and achieving those goals—*or even making measurable progress toward those goals*—leads to this feeling.

Would you like to be in a situation where you work only because you want to and not because you must? We call that state of being "financial independence." **If you like the sound of that, then this book is for you.**

In the pages that follow, I will outline a path for you to more efficiently reach your financial goals, and to achieve financial independence years sooner. Your chances of success, and therefore greater happiness, are multiplied by a good working knowledge of personal finance, and a long list of insider's tips on the investment industry and financial planning.

I promise to provide this information in a straightforward, efficient manner and in everyday language that you can understand. You may find many of the concepts to be common sense, once you fully understand them, and that's great. If we can help you cut through the crap—the conflicting, self-serving information that is constantly being fed to you—you can make better decisions in all areas of your life, and avoid costly mistakes.

My goal is to help you be happier by being more successful, on your terms. So the first thing we have to do is help you figure out what's really important to you. If you always feel you are pursuing **your own** goals, and not someone else's, you will find that pursuit easier, and can approach it with much more passion.

Research has proven that people who set specific, measurable goals and develop an achievable plan to reach them may be up to 97% more likely to achieve them than people who do not.

Introduction

MOST FINANCIAL BOOKS start in the middle, rather than at the beginning. They focus on products, the economy, the stock market, sometimes on global issues and trends, demographics and financial tactics. Some promise to show you how to beat the stock market. Some focus on getting out of debt, while others on esoteric topics like how to buy real estate with no money down, or how to avoid the upcoming economic cataclysm.

A few of these books are very well written, practical and could be a great help for you in refining and implementing your financial plan. We provide a list of these in our appendix, and mention some throughout this book.

Managing the Bull starts at the beginning, and it focuses on you. What is your purpose? What do you want to achieve using these products, tactics and investment "secrets"?

Most financial books ignore the fact that every person is unique. Some people want to be rich, others just want to be comfortable so they can pursue their passions, while others could care less about material things but want to make a positive difference in the world. Some want to live a life of greater significance. Many want to retire early, some of them to a warmer climate.

The secret to success and happiness is identifying your purpose early, making the vision real and specific, and then developing an implementable process to reach each of the successive milestones contained in a proper plan.

When the plan begins to be implemented, it's important that it remains fresh, relevant and accurate. This requires a renewal process, which includes reconfirming the long-term goals, measuring the progress towards them, updating the milestones and adjusting the overall plan accordingly.

These are the true secrets to achieving your personal and financial goals. The implementation of the plan is very important, and we will talk about it throughout the book, and give you some insights that will allow you to sidestep the crap—**the Bull**—that the media and financial industry try to throw your way. But my 30 years of helping people achieve their goals tell me that the most important step—**by far**—is developing a clear, compelling vision of your future, and writing down specific, measurable goals that will move you toward that compelling future.

Need a bit more proof?

Our financial planning practice looks after 75 families. Most of them started out with nothing other than some skills and ambition. Now, the vast majority of our clients are financially independent, growing their assets and only working if they choose to do so.

We call our unique method *The Goal Achiever Process*™ and that's what it does. And it works. We have always focused on helping clients define, refine and achieve their goals, and that's a key reason for their success, and for ours.

As completely independent advisors, paid only by our clients, we also know more than anyone else about the dissection of investment products and strategies, and how to minimize costs and maximize returns. Those are the secrets we will share with you.

I'm very excited about helping you on your life's journey. Thanks for the opportunity!

Part 1

Ignore the Bull:
Plan Your Own Path to
Financial Independence

Sometimes I think life is just a rodeo,
The trick is to ride and make it to the bell.

- J.C. FOGERTY, 1985

1

How do *You* Define Success and Then Focus on What Matters to You?

TWO STORIES HAVE HAD A BIG EFFECT on the way I look at life, and on determining what's most important to me. See if they have the same effect on you:

The big rocks[1]

A teacher filled a jar with large stones and asked the students if the jar was full. Most said "yes."

He then poured sand into the jar, filling the gaps. He again asked the students, some of whom had caught on and said "probably not."

Then came the water, which the teacher poured slowly into the gaps between the grains of sand.

The students were then satisfied the jar was full, but were amazed at the way the experience had tested their perceptions. One said, "If I start with the small stuff, I'll have no room left."

Aha.

The same is true with life. Figure out what the big rocks are in your life first, and make room for those.

There will always be space for the less important things.

---

[1] This is a variation of the parable first written by Stephen R. Covey, with A. Roger Merrill and Rebecca Merrill, *First Things First*, Simon and Schuster (1995).

The carpenter

There was an elderly carpenter who was poised to retire.

He told his employer-contractor of his plans to leave the house building business and live a more leisurely life with his wife, enjoying his extended family. He would miss the paycheque, but he needed to retire. Financially, they could get by.

The contractor was sorry to see his exceptional worker go and asked if he could build just one more house as a personal favour. The carpenter said yes, but in time it was easy to see that his heart was not in his work. He resorted to shoddy workmanship and used inferior materials.

It was a sad way to end a dedicated and distinguished career.

When the carpenter finished his work, the employer came to inspect the house. He handed the front-door key to the carpenter. "This is your house," he said, "my gift to you."

The carpenter was shocked and grateful but quickly thought, "What a shame!" If he had only known he was building his own house, he would have done it all so differently.

So it is with us. We build our lives, a day at a time, often putting less than our best into the building. Then with a shock we realize we have to live in the house we have built. If we could do it over, we might do it much differently.

But we cannot go back.

You are the carpenter. Each day you hammer a nail, place a board, or erect a wall. "Life is a do-it-yourself project," someone has said.

Your attitudes and the choices you make today build the "house" you live in tomorrow. Build wisely!

2

What is Your Vision of Your Future?

ARE YOU ABLE TO IDENTIFY your most cherished values? Can you say what you would really want—*or need*—to achieve in your life?

That's a tough one for most people. Recently, a client told me that he had always felt his mission in life was to help people be happier by giving them the means and the knowledge to reach their goals. He obviously found his calling as a financial advisor. (Yes, I have financial advisors as clients. Everyone needs a coach, and even experts can benefit from another point of view.)

If you are already as clear as that on what you want from your life, that's fabulous. Take five minutes now and write out your mission, and then add as much detail as you possibly can.

For many of us, however, it takes a long time to really know what is most important. If that statement is true for you, that's okay. In the meantime, though, it may be possible to still set some very specific—and very important—goals.

Let's start to develop a compelling vision of your ideal future. **Close your eyes and picture yourself in the future, financially independent and secure. Take a few minutes to fully appreciate how you feel.**

Are you relaxed? Do you feel confident and safe?

Where are you? What are you doing? Who is with you? Is there a warm breeze blowing on your face?

Again, how do you *feel*?

Are you aware of the sounds? Listen for them.

Focus for a minute on how everything smells.

Did you see yourself on a beach? In your garden? On a golf course? Or maybe you're on a ski hill, or swimming in the ocean.

Maybe you are in your own home, but with more time to do the things that you really want to do.

Take a few minutes to refine that vision, until it is truly yours and you can really feel it, hear it, smell it and even taste it. When you think you have developed a compelling picture of your future, write down as many details as you can.

A great way to do this is with, "I am...." statements. Some examples:

- I am walking with my wife, talking and laughing.
- I am debt free.
- I am in great physical shape—strong and flexible.
- I am feeling confident about my present, and my future.
- I am the supervisor at work.
- I am running my own business.
- I am physically active.
- I am (golfing, jogging, skiing, sailing, reading)....
- I am learning....
- I am working three days per week.
- I am in Kenya, doing volunteer work.
- I am lounging on a beach.

Develop as much detail as you can, and make it your own. This is not about other people's expectations or goals. It is all about yours. Let yourself be selfish.

And don't worry about being realistic. Let yourself have big goals. In fact, go ahead and develop some B-HAGs, what Jim Collins and Jerry Porras call Big Hairy Audacious Goals[2]. In business, these are the kinds of goals that have transformed industries, or caused the invention of new ones.

Henry Ford's transformative goal was to, "Democratize the automobile." Microsoft decided it wanted to facilitate "a computer on every desk and in every home"; Amazon had the ridiculous concept of, "Every book, ever printed, in any language, all available in 60 seconds." (While they were at it, they would also be "Earth's most customer centric company.")

All were crazy ideas at the time, but embracing those audacious goals forced these companies to think in new ways, invent new ways of doing things, and set higher standards for service.

In your case, you may decide that you have to double your income in order to reach your goals. How do you do that? Does it mean going back to school to get a university degree? Does it mean going into sales, in an industry where very high

---

[2] James C. Collins and Jerry I. Porras, *Built to Last: Successful Habits of Visionary Companies*. Harper Collins (1994).

incomes are achievable? Does it mean taking on a second job temporarily, until you achieve certain milestones?

Maybe your big goals just take more time. Something that is not achievable in three years might be possible in five years, or even ten. That may seem like a long time, but it's the blink of an eye in the context of the rest of your life. And take it from an old guy, it is incredible how quickly five years can pass by.

Now, back to your vision of your future... really put yourself in that picture, as strongly and vividly as you can. Now create two thoughts or details that you can conjure up any time, to place you back in the picture, to feel those positive feelings, and to help you remember why you are making the positive choices you'll need to make going forward.

These thoughts are your anchors and your positive voice, which you can draw upon for motivation when things get tough, or when you need help making the right choices to achieve your future vision, instead of just enjoying a fleeting pleasure.

3

Developing Your Winner's Mindset

TO GIVE YOU A VISCERAL FEEL for the Winner's Mindset that will propel you to a great future, step one is to start appreciating your progress and achievements.

Take your pencil and paper and, looking back over the past year, write down all of the good things that have happened and all the progress you have made toward your longer-term goals.

Next, make a list—***right now***—of the things for which you feel grateful. For the sake of this exercise, you have permission to ignore any shortcomings or mistakes, or to simply use them as a learning tool. Do not dwell on them, or obsess about any regrets.

For example, one of your goals in the year past might have been to pay off all debts. Let's say you didn't make it. Celebrate the progress you made and use that as your starting point for looking ahead.

Maybe you paid off some debts, but incurred others. What did you learn from that?

It's also possible you slid backwards on some things. If that's the truth, then acknowledge it, but also find the areas where you have moved forward. Make that list as long as you can, including all areas of your life, not just money.

Remember, life is about progress, not perfection. Perfection is unattainable.[3] Develop the habit of celebrating your progress.

Now, how can you make this coming year even more successful than your last?

---

[3] Dan Sullivan, coach and co-founder with Babs Smith of *The Strategic Coach® Program* (1988).

What do you really want to accomplish this year? What do you want to eliminate?

While you have your pencil out, grab another piece of paper and make two lists:

1. Things I always wanted to do.
2. Things I never want to do again.

If you have a life partner, have that person complete these lists, as well, and compare. Get excited together about any areas of common ground, and also get excited about your partner's unique hopes and dreams.

What did you find out that you didn't know? How can you help that person's progress? Are there any immediate steps you can take toward the life you want?

Now comes the fun part—freeing yourself to dream about what you want your life to be like in one, three and five years, or beyond. Just start thinking, and write things down as they come to you. Don't worry at this point about being too structured; that can come later. **The job right now is to make your future vision as big as you dare, and then as real and as compelling as you can.** Add in details to make it come alive.

Close your eyes and walk your future self through a perfect day, and write down as much detail about that day as you can.

4

SMART No Bull Goals

WHEN YOUR FUTURE VISION is sufficiently gripping and undeniable, it is time to turn it into specific, measurable and time-bound goals. These are the specific first steps, and future milestones along the way that will help you design your financial and life plan and then measure your progress and your success.

I keep talking about pencil and paper, rather than computer, and here's why. Writing down specific goals is vital for several reasons. When you write them down, your brain goes to work on them immediately in the subconscious, finding ways to accomplish them.

Adding your key goals and anchors to your mobile device, screensaver or wall is also a great idea, and I encourage that. But I really think it is important to physically write out your dreams and plans, to help hardwire them into your brain.

Writing your goals down several times is that much more effective. So, rewrite your list and your plans as often as you can, refining them each time. Make them increasingly specific and measurable. SMART goals are *specific, measurable, attainable, realistic* and *time-bound*.[4]

I am big on the specific, measurable and timely. I'm not so hung up on attainable and realistic, though I think that **the first steps** in your plan must always be realistic and achievable. It's those first steps that are critical.

Remember, of course, that it is the **execution** of your plan—the actions you take and the choices you make over time—that will actually get you there.

---

4   G. T. Doran, "There's a S.M.A.R.T. way to write management's goals and objectives," *Management Review*, (1981) Volume 70, Issue 11 (AMA FORUM), pp. 35-36.

Making your vision powerful and compelling is the most important step. The next is to write down a specific plan and the daily, weekly and monthly steps you need to take to make it happen.

Research suggests that when you combine this detailed planning with writing down specific goals, your chance of success goes up from 3% to about 90%. How do I know this?

Harvard University MBA program graduates in 1979 were asked, "Have you set clear, written goals for your future and made plans to accomplish them?"

Only 3% of the grad students had written goals and plans, while 13% said they had goals but they were not in writing. Fully 84% had no specific goals at all.

When interviewed 10 years later, the results were remarkable. The 13% who had specific, unwritten goals were earning, on average, twice as much as the group with no specific goals.

Same sample, same education—twice as much income. Pretty impressive. But, as they say on the infomercials—Wait! There's more!

Incredibly, the 3% with written, specific goals were earning an average of 10 times as much as the other 97% put together!

This research appears in the seminal book *What They Don't Teach You at Harvard Business School*, by Mark H. McCormack.[5] It's an important read, even today.

There is a ton of great material on goal setting in every bookstore and on the internet. I encourage you to review some of this, and to embrace specific, written goal setting as a way of life, in all areas of yours.

It is vital to make your life a conscious decision. Write down what you want and craft your plan to get it. Then start today... and make this coming year the best year ever!

---

[5]   Mark H. McCormack, *What They Don't Teach You at Harvard Business School*. Bantam Books (1986).

5

How Will *You* Define
Financial Independence?

"SURE, HE'S GOT A BIG HAT, but he's got no cattle."

I attribute that quote to two authors named Thomas J. Stanley and William D. Danko, from their book *The Millionaire Next Door*[6] which I read many years ago. They say that "Big hat, no cattle" is a traditional Texas saying used to describe someone who has a lot of show but no real substance, especially financial substance.

In non-agricultural terms, we would say that person has use of a lot of material things, but very little equity built up in them. Someone with two fancy leased cars, a big house with a big mortgage, consumer loans and very few investments might appear very rich and successful to someone on the outside. But has that person achieved any real wealth?

Let's muse a little about what constitutes a reasonable measure of wealth and how we might think about the term "financial independence."

We use the term financial independence when talking to clients, as opposed to retirement. We define it as **the time when you can live off your investments and the equity you have built up, rather than having to work for pay**.

In other words, it is the point at which you are able to choose to work for your own reasons, rather than just economic needs.

The key to this is developing passive income from things like savings, non-registered investments, Tax Free Savings Accounts (TFSAs), Registered Retirement Savings Plans (RRSPs and RRIFs), pensions, annuities, business assets, rental real estate or less common things like royalty income.

---

[6] Thomas J. Stanley and William D. Danko, *The Millionaire Next Door: The Surprising Secrets of America's Wealthy*. Longstreet Press (1996).

In *The Millionaire Next Door,* they roughly define wealth as your equity divided by your annual expenses. If your net worth—all of your assets minus your liabilities—is $1 million and your annual living expenses are $50,000, then the ratio of equity to expenses is 20 to 1. That's wealthy.

On the other hand, if your equity is $200,000 and it costs you $100,000 each year to live, then your equity to expense ratio is only two to one. That means you could only last two years without working before your net worth would be exhausted—**not** wealthy.

That second example might be someone who makes an awful lot of money and lives very well, but has "no cattle."

You can further refine this formula by only counting income-producing assets and leaving out personal use assets.

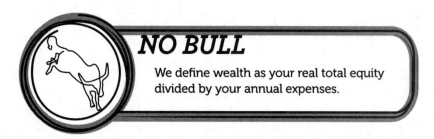

NO BULL

We define wealth as your real total equity divided by your annual expenses.

Years ago, I glanced briefly at another book called *The Six-Day Financial Makeover* by California-based financial advisor Robert Pagliarini.[7]

Here is a quote his publicist sent along, when she wanted me to review the book: "Financial independence involves earning enough passive income to support the lifestyle you desire, and the first thing to do is make the distinction between this and your current lifestyle. It is not about limiting or reducing your current lifestyle, using credit cards or taking out other loans. It is about living the life you want and having the means to support it... when income generated by your assets can fully support your expenses."

Exactly!

We encourage our clients who are not yet retired to define their current expense needs and then review them in the context of having more leisure time. Some costs will go down significantly: retirement savings, pension contributions, some of the costs of going to work, like transportation and clothing, Canada Pension Plan and Employment Insurance premiums, maybe even the need for two cars.

---

7 Robert Pagliarini, *The Six-Day Financial Makeover: Transform Your Financial Life in Less Than a Week.* St. Martin's Press (2006).

On the other hand, some costs may go up, like travel, hobbies, golf, home improvements and other activities you hope to increase with your bountiful leisure time.

Having a very clear picture of your future income needs is a critical first component of calculating your financial independence need. It is then a fairly simple matter for you—or your financial planner—to determine the amount of capital (the sources of future passive income) that you will need to achieve that need.

Your planner can also help you determine the amount of savings that you need to produce each year, based on a safe assumption of rate of return and future inflation.

Even if inflation continues to average only 2% per year, it means the income you need in the future **will still double every 36 years**. You likely hope to be retired for 36 years and that's not unreasonable. Our most distinguished client just turned 95, while another one passed away at 104!

If inflation averages 3%, then expenses will double in just 24 years. None of this includes the possibility of significant healthcare costs adding to retirement income needs.

If you have a pension, you have a huge head start on the rest of us, who must amass the capital all on our own.

Traditionally, financial planners have used a figure of 70% of pre-retirement income as a target for retirement. For some people that fits, but for many it is either too high or too low. Debates rage among planners, actuaries and pundits about whether the financial services industry is purposely scaring people into saving too much or, conversely, whether we financial planners are actually allowing people to be too complacent and risk never having enough to achieve financial independence.

A study prepared by the Canadian Institute of Actuaries on age 40-something Canadians suggests that many of these "late boomers" are far behind on their savings and that up to two-thirds will have trouble paying for the basic necessities in retirement.[8]

There are many big hats out there apparently, and not a lot of cattle herds.

If that sounds a little scary, so be it. I hope that it will motivate you to sit down and develop a clear picture of your desired lifestyle at financial independence, the income needed to support that lifestyle and the financial plan you will need to get there.

Don't be part of that group that waited too long and is now left behind, or dependent on governments, family or charity for their retirement needs.

---

[8]   Canadian Association of Actuaries, *Planning for Retirement: Are Canadians Saving Enough*; 2007.

6

The Art and the Science of Setting Goals

AS I'VE SAID, **your goals and objectives should be SMART—specific, measurable, achievable, relevant and time-bound.**

It helps if you can develop a specific plan to take you from here to there. That means moving from your accurate current snapshot of where you are today to that situation you have vividly visualized for your future.

Once again, **close your eyes and visualize yourself as financially independent.** What does that mean to you? What does it look like? How do you feel? Put vivid details in your picture, details that use all of your senses. (Go ahead; I'll wait.)

Now let's start to make it concrete and achievable.

Let's say your financial independence requires $40,000 per year of income from investments, protected from inflation. You will therefore need to have $1,000,000 in 25 years. To reach that dream you will need to invest about $1,300 per month at a 7% return.

This process applies to all of your life goals, not just financial. If you want to lose 24 pounds over the next year, then you have to lose two pounds per month, or one half pound per week. This might mean eating 300 fewer calories per day than you burn up.

I also strongly believe that writing down your goals is very important and that going "public" with them can strengthen your commitment to them. Remember, it is the strength of your vision and commitment to yourself that will carry you over the inevitable obstacles.

See if you can visualize a huge future for yourself, even one that you cannot see realistically attaining.

If you can make that vision powerful enough and your commitment strong enough, you will find a way to get there.

SMART Goal Worksheet and Example

First, state your intention with your goal. This is a general comment on what you want to achieve.

> **My Intention—***Pay off all consumer debts other than mortgage, to free up monthly cash flow for investing, and to feel more in control of my finances.*

Next, make sure your goals answer all of these questions:

1. **Specific—***What specifically will I do? How will I do it? How will I measure achievement?*
    - I will pay off all non-mortgage consumer debt within 12 months. I will divide my outstanding debts, plus interest, by 12, to determine total monthly payments needed. I will set up an automatic transfer from my chequing account to the loans, so extra payments are made each payday.
    - I will not use my credit cards or line of credit, or otherwise sabotage my prospects for success.

2. **Measurable—***How will I measure success?*
    - By December 31, 2013, the outstanding balance on my line of credit, credit cards and furniture loan will all be zero, and no new debts will have replaced them.

3. **Achievable—***Can I do this?*
    - What adjustments will I have to make to my spending? Will I need more income? Can I pay the debts off even faster by making some additional good choices?

4. **Relevant—***Is achievement of this goal important to what I want to ultimately achieve?*
    - By freeing up $500 per month of cash flow by eliminating debt payments, I can then invest $400 of this and put $100 toward the (gym membership/ guitar lesson/music library/etc.) that I want. The $400 added to my RRSP contribution will reduce my taxes by $1,800, which I can also invest.

5. **Time-based—***Is there a specific date attached to achievement? Have I set up appropriate milestones along the way to measure progress?*
    - December 31, 2013 is my achievement date. I will measure my progress monthly, to ensure I am on track. If I fall short, I will increase payments in the following month to catch up.

Exciting, isn't it?

If your previous "goal setting" has consisted of "I wish..." statements, this new approach will be tremendously empowering for you.

Take some time now to complete your own SMART Goals using this handy worksheet.

SMART Goal Worksheet

Today's Date: _____ Target Date: _____

Start Date: _____ Date Achieved: _____

Goal: _____

1. **Specific**: *What **exactly** will I accomplish?*

_____

_____

2. **Measurable**: *How will I know when I have achieved success with this goal?*

_____

_____

3. **Achievable**: *Is achieving this goal realistic with effort and commitment? Do I have the resources to achieve this goal? If not, how—or where—will I get them?*

_____

_____

4. **Relevant**: *Why is this goal significant to my life and to what I want to achieve?*

_____

_____

5. **Timely**: *What is my deadline to achieve success with this goal?*

_____

_____

continued...

This goal is important because:

_____

_____

The benefits of achieving this goal will be:

_____

_____

Potential Obstacles   **Potential Solutions**

_____   _____

_____   _____

_____   _____

_____   _____

_____   _____

Who are the people I will ask to help me?

_____

_____

Specific Action Steps: *What steps need to be taken to get me to my goal?*

What?	Expected Completion Date	Completed
_____	_____	☐
_____	_____	☐
_____	_____	☐
_____	_____	☐
_____	_____	☐

7

Wait a Minute—
Is There a Tough Part
Coming Up?

I GUESS WE'VE PUT THIS OFF LONG ENOUGH... is Christianson actually talking about making tough choices, and maybe even sacrifices?

Yeah, that might be the case. But really, how big a sacrifice is having last year's phone model, or a three year old car, or having a "staycation" once every few years?

As North Americans, we are so spoiled in our lifestyles, it borders on the absurd. People are starving around the world; billions of people do not even have a roof over their heads. Six billion people do not have access to clean water. And we complain that our 36 inch TV is too small and fails to display *Men in Black* in 3D.

It's all about perspective, and keeping yours. Let me give you an example.

I spent ten years advising NHL hockey players on their money and, to some extent, on their lives. When they reached the NHL, most of the ones I met were good, solid, hardworking young men, who had toiled many years to reach the pinnacle, and appreciated everything they now had. But it was hard for some to keep that perspective.

I remember a very young Saskatchewan lad—we'll call him Brett—who had been drafted by the Senators, and was trying to get his bearings in this new world. We were having dinner, and he asked, among a slew of other charmingly naïve questions, "How many cars should I own?" My initial internal response was, of course, "Huh?" but I needed to know what was behind the thinking, so I asked Brett, "What do you mean?"

His answer was that, on the farm, they just had the vehicles they needed, but now his Russian linemate had seven cars, and was shopping for another. "What's the 'right number' for me?" It wasn't a greed question, it turned out, but instead just a desire to learn, to fit in, and to do what was right and appropriate in this new world.

It was a long, wonderful dinner and, I think, a very important one for that rookie. We talked about common sense, what motivates some people to do silly things, and what was truly important to Brett. We talked about goals and purpose. We talked about long term plans and short term concerns. We talked about making your own choices, being your own person, and modeling the behaviours of the **right** people.

It turned out that his number one value was his family, and his desire to help them with their struggling farm was his first goal. Second was to become financially independent as soon as he could, because he knew his career could be over any time. He wanted to take advantage of his good fortune now, to make sure his and his family's future would be secure. We worked on a plan to reach those goals as quickly as possible.

As of this writing, Brett still earns $4 million a year in the NHL. The farm is debt free thanks to his support, and thriving as a result. He has long since achieved financial independence, and now gives back much of his time and money to the community and the world. He has been married to the same woman since his third year in the league. He still only has three vehicles, including an old Ford F150 on the farm. He's happy.

Other players I met were never happy. One held out on his $4.5 million contract because a rival had signed for $5 million. Others had to go on a shopping spree in every city in which they played.

The Russian linemate was in debt—though he did have 13 cars—when he was cut from the team two years later and lost his salary. He now sells cars. Others are on their third or fourth wives.

Many tried to fill a psychological gap with material things. They never found out what was really important to **them**.

Those players—like many of us—had no real perspective on how good things were and no understanding of just how lucky they were.

Do you?

Even if you feel poor in Canada, your lifestyle puts you in the top 5% of people in the world. If you are a middle income earner in Canada, you are in the top 3% of people in the entire world. That's not bad.

Out of all the great lines and quotes I heard in the hockey business, my absolute favourite came as I was driving three players from the (then) Corel Centre in Kanata, to downtown Ottawa for some drinks on Elgin Street. The mood was a bit subdued after a loss, and 45 minutes on the stationery bikes after the game.

Suddenly from the back seat, 37-year-old Grant Ledyard yelled, "Hey, what time is it?"

As the young fellas struggled to look at their watches, Winnipeg-born Ledyard answered his own question. *"It's the time of your f*&*ing life, and don't forget it."*

That attitude, and the commitment to spend 45 minutes in the gym AFTER playing 33 minutes in an NHL game in his 16th season in the league, told me why he had lasted so long in the NHL, in a young man's game where a thousand talented players want your job every day.

What does that teach us?

Appreciating what you have is free, AND priceless. If you appreciate what you have, you will enjoy happiness today, and also possess the energy and attitude to make your life continually better in the future.

You will always be improving, but remember, right NOW is always the time of your life. Don't forget it.

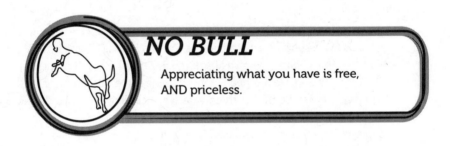

NO BULL

Appreciating what you have is free,
AND priceless.

8

Your Agenda or Theirs?

EITHER YOU HAVE YOUR OWN AGENDA, or you are destined to follow someone else's. That's another great reason for you to have your own powerful vision of the future, and to develop the knowledge of what it takes to get you there.

There are billions of dollars being paid in advertising to encourage you to part with your money, on consumer goods and services, experiences, consumables and investments. We want you to be informed and clear about your chosen future and your current needs so that you can sift through all the marketing material and find what's right for you.

Here's a suggestion for your financial success: the absolutely coolest thing you can obtain—*the ultimate, selfish luxury*—is **surplus cash**.

Forget the iPad, forget carbon fiber golf clubs and designer sushi, ignore the call of the Maserati and trips to Cancun or South Beach.

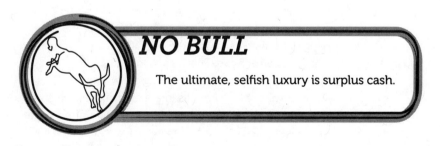

NO BULL

The ultimate, selfish luxury is surplus cash.

Sure, those things make you feel great for a few moments in time, like you're the coolest kid on the block or a master of the universe. But the feeling doesn't last, and very soon you need another fix.

I am telling you that the most powerful and lasting luxury good—the one that permanently relieves stress, increases your confidence in every aspect of your life and makes you irresistible to the opposite sex—is surplus cash flow.

That's right, spending less than you make and keeping your total financial commitments below your net income will make you feel better than a weekly trip to the spa for their best cucumber eye treatment, mud wrap and thorough pampering.

It's better—and WAY cooler—than a daily trip to Starbucks, leaving Victoria's Secret or the Apple store with an armful of goods, or going to an all-inclusive you can't afford.

Even a slight surplus can have these powerful effects, and create an irresistible charisma—an aura, if you will—around a person who formerly appeared nervous, awkward or possibly as annoying as Bobcat Goldthwait.

That nervousness and preoccupation is what happens to people when they are wondering if they will make it to the next paycheque, juggling credit cards and overdraft payments, all the while fretting that their iPhone is already last year's model and now so uncool. (Don't even get me started on the negative health effects of such a stress-filled situation.)

So, how do we re-brand surplus cash flow as the coolest thing a person can have, and the ultimate luxury good?

Let me draw an analogy with surplus time: Everyone knows what it's like to be running behind schedule, rushing to important appointments, worrying about being late, not having time to prepare or find a legal parking place, and constantly apologizing.

The opposite is when you allow extra time to get somewhere. You have time to drive around and find a free parking space, have time to check your texts and emails after you have actually parked the car (as opposed to doing it in traffic), can take a few moments for yourself and even prepare properly for the important meeting about to take place.

It is a wonderful luxury, and one that can completely change the way you feel about yourself. Having extra time can also provide a 100% improvement in how you perform, and what you can achieve. That's good for you.

Having extra cash works the same way as having extra time.

A deficit causes borrowing, which creates interest payments, which gets you further behind. Surplus cash allows you to avoid interest, and often negotiate a better price on things when you are able to pay cash. Or, you have the luxury of using credit cards and earning points, and then paying them off in full every month, while you hang onto your cash.

Surplus money can be saved to buy those desirable luxury goods **with cash**, pay for vacations in advance so they can be truly enjoyed without guilt or worry, and allow other stress-relieving activities like buying Christmas presents before December 24.

Ultimately, your cash surplus can be invested for the future, allowing achievement of your most important goals.

If used for Registered Retirement Savings Plan contributions, it can also reduce current income taxes.

As that long-term nest egg multiplies and financial independence approaches at an earlier age, a person's confidence grows, along with the ever-increasing freedom to take time off from work, change careers, and take once-in-a-lifetime adventures and experience all manner of other luxuries that most people never achieve.

Sound good?

9

Spot the Bull

I WANT YOU TO BECOME your own consumer vigilante, or at least a vigilant consumer.

Many people still buy things on credit without considering the real costs.

My son Taylor pointed this out to me once at a young age while he was doing his daily reading of the computer ads. Computer prices had plummeted and the advertised totals were very attractive, but he happened to multiply out the monthly lease cost by the term of the lease and came up with a much bigger dollar figure.

He did not think this could possibly be right.

I suggested that he calculate the difference as a percentage of the original sale price. The additional cost was 38% if you "rented" it on a three-year lease, compared to purchasing it with cash.

Thirty-eight percent!

In other words, a $1,799 computer was going to cost $2,484 (plus buyout after three years) if paid on a lease. So much for the "new lower price."

And, as Taylor pointed out, the computer would be obsolete before it was paid off. (That may be the good news because the buyout amount is based on fair market value at that time.)

This was not some fly-by-night computer company, but one of the largest in the world. The experience reminds us to check the full price and the interest rate before leasing or borrowing. (This company will also be happy to finance a conventional purchase over four years, but they will charge 18.99% interest each year.)

Car leasing can also be very expensive, especially because leasing allows you to "afford" a lot more car than you could otherwise swing. This has tempted many consumers down the road to Corinthian leather and Bluetooth connectivity.

Remember that when you lease, you only borrow to buy a portion of the car that you will be using over the term of the lease. For example, if the car costs $30,000 and it is expected to be worth $15,000 in three years, then essentially you borrow $15,000 from the leasing company. They still own the car, so you must give it back at the end of the lease or buy it from them for the $15,000 buyout fee.

You are usually paying a premium interest rate on the amount you borrow, and, of course, you don't build any equity. Your payments simply cover the depreciation.

A much smarter idea is to buy a two or three-year old car (that may have just come off lease) that may still have warranty. Then you pay the $15,000 (hopefully with cash) and you're done. Even if you borrow, your payments will be roughly the same as leasing a new car and after three years, you'll OWN a car worth probably $10,000.

Get in the habit of letting someone else pay for the depreciation and the extra $10,000 for their "new car smell," which you can actually buy in a bottle for $7.99.

Furniture, electronics, and other consumer goods are seducing many people into spending money they don't yet have. If you can get in the habit of setting goals for things you want and then saving the money to purchase the items you want with cash, you've taken 10 steps forward in your financial planning.

You will be much further ahead as a consumer and you will follow a much faster route to your own financial independence.

Managing the Bull:
Detect and Deflect the Crap

REMEMBER, you are looking to follow your own path to financial independence. Don't let the "crap" get in your way. Before we move on to the next part of your journey, let's review some of the ways you can detect and deflect the crap:

- Always wanting something you don't have—or craving things you will never afford—is a guaranteed recipe for unhappiness.

- Appreciating what you have is the secret ingredient to both being happy AND to achieving and attaining those things you don't have. Gratitude and happiness equal power and effectiveness, in achieving your goals.

- This does not mean settling—it just means appreciating.

- Striving for goals and achieving the progress that comes from that positive striving takes you to the next level of happiness.

- Your likelihood of success can be multiplied hugely by mastering the skill of setting SMART goals, and exercising that skill to set specific, measurable and exciting goals that continually energize you.

- None of us can have everything. Each goal brings with it choices. By making the choices that move you toward your goals—even when this means delaying shallow but immediate gratification—you will achieve much more in your life, and enjoy much greater happiness along the way. This statement is true when it applies to your health, diet, exercise, relationships and, of course, money.

- Be smart about your choices, and don't fall victim to the seduction of the advertising industry and the corporate agenda. Realize that holding onto your money until you can afford what you want will help you in every aspect of your life.

- Think about surplus cash as being the ultimate luxury good. Test drive it and you'll see.

Above all, remember that your life, your happiness and your future are in your hands. Make the right choices for you.

Part 2

Riding the Bull: Making Money Work for You

(Making it work) takes a little longer
(Making it work) takes a little time...
- DOUG BENNET, DOUG AND THE SLUGS, 1983

10

How Money Works—
Income from Work vs.
Income from Capital

OK, LET'S MAKE YOU SOME MONEY...

This section of the book is divided into two main themes—how to accumulate and then invest capital to make it grow, and how to assemble the right team to help you reach your goals and dreams.

First, though, a review of why you accumulate capital.

We're all familiar with the term "capitalism," but have we thought about what capitalism really means, and how it is important for us and our goals?

Income from work

We all know what it's like to work for a living and be paid by the hour. It is very difficult to get ahead. Someone else is the boss, and calls the shots. Saving any significant money to invest is a big challenge. It's also tough to visualize the situation changing in the short term.

As we advance in our careers and income increases, things typically improve, and there is more discretionary income with which to save and invest, and perhaps more company-supported savings and retirement plans. It's easier to see that one day the savings and investments will pay off.

Those developments are certainly evolutionary rather than revolutionary. The constant demand to work for income—both to pay for the basics of living and the extras like vacations that make it all worthwhile—continues. The need to put away long-term investments for retirement also remains.

This is the reality for most people, and we will focus on how to make this work. However, it's very important to keep the long-term transition—from toil to leisure—in mind.

Income from capital

Eventually, there comes a time when accumulated investments become adequate to replace the income from your own personal toil. This accumulated capital could be in the form of RRSPs, pension plans, non-registered savings, TFSAs, real estate investments or a variety of other forms of capital that can produce income.

Accumulating this capital might be facilitated by your monthly savings and astute investments, or it might come from inheritance or perhaps the ownership of a business.

The important concept is that you achieve financial independence when your capital can produce enough income to support your lifestyle. At that point, you can then make a decision to work or not, based on your personal needs and desires, rather than on economic demands.

When you are financially independent, you are only working because you *want* to work.

That is *my* vision for you, and my reason for writing this book: to help you achieve financial independence more quickly and in a way that puts *you* in control, making your own conscious choices and reaping the rewards.

The path to achieving this nirvanic state has three main components, or phases:

1. Accumulating investment capital, through saving from regular income, reducing income taxes, controlling spending, building equity in a business, producing something of value that people will buy, and/or inheriting capital.
2. Making that capital grow, through the disciplined application of an appropriate investment policy, likely for many years.
3. Gradually converting that growth capital into vehicles that will produce regular income, when needed, in a tax-effective manner.

In most cases, the accumulation phase will take patience, and therefore discipline—sticking to a smart process.

NO BULL

When you are financially independent, you are only working because you *want* to work.

11

Harness Your Power

A VERY WISE CLIENT said to me recently, "I don't have any poor friends." I asked why he thought that was, and he said, without hesitation: "They don't spend very much." ***They have always spent less than they made.***

This wise man is 70, has been financially independent for at least a decade, and still works full time because he loves his work. Now, obviously, a 70-year-old is going to have a lot more financially independent friends than you will. But the profound simplicity of what he said struck me.

Many of his friends have been friends since childhood. They all grew up in a poor part of town, born to poor parents. Many are now staggeringly wealthy.

Coincidence?

When you are earning income from employment, the only way to move toward financial independence is to spend less than you make. There is really no shortcut.

Yes, you want to make better investments and achieve a better rate of return. You want to take advantage of any company-sponsored retirement plans that can add to your savings capacity. And you want to become eligible for stock options or

NO BULL

When you are earning income from employment, the only way to move toward financial independence is to spend less than you make. There is really no shortcut.

other equity participation plans as soon as you can, so that you can participate in the capital appreciation of the company.

You may also want to start your own business, and build up equity value much faster by being a capitalist, while providing value to customers. It is that equity play that will help you achieve financial independence at a relatively young age.

Those are all great goals, but all of them require capital to achieve. For almost everyone, the only way to build up capital initially is to save it. Even if your plan is to borrow to invest or to start a company, your lender will insist on your having some initial equity.

The sooner you build up that cash reserve and then turn it into an appropriate investment portfolio, the sooner you will be benefiting from compound interest and the flexibility that equity gives you.

The key to much of everything we've talked about so far comes down to that one concept—*pay yourself first.*

Before you commit to any other form of expense, commit to paying yourself. Start with a minimum of 10% of your paycheque—*preferably 10% of the gross and not of the net*—and set up an automatic savings and investment plan for that money.

If you can commit to 15% or 20%, all the better.

You can't tell me that you think your landlord, mortgage lender, Visa card issuer, car dealer, furniture store or electronics outlet are more deserving than you, right?

Can you give me one good reason why you think it's more important that you help them achieve **their** profit targets, rather than you achieving your own financial independence?

NO BULL

Pay yourself first.

If not, then let's make a commitment, right here and now, to always make sure that you get paid first.

Strategy number one is to set up automatic transfers from your chequing or operating account into investments. Ideally, time these transfers to coincide with your paydays, so your personal investments have first access to your income, prior to all the other demands on it.

Mutual fund investments lend themselves well to this approach. They have low minimum monthly investment amounts of as little as $50, as long as these are set up through a Pre-authorized Cheque Plan (or PAC), which automatically draws money from your account and places it in the investment fund of your choice.

Investing fixed dollar amounts like this on a regular basis also gives you a slight mathematical advantage when investing into a vehicle with fluctuating values, like an equity mutual fund. In months when the market is down, you purchase more units or shares with your fixed amount of dollars. This means you buy low, to a limited extent.

When the market is high, you purchase slightly fewer units with your fixed dollars. This concept of "Dollar Cost Averaging" can help with accumulating capital. Even more important, though, is the regularity and consistency of investing. Especially in extended bear markets, this can be a benefit, as you keep accumulating fund units or shares at lower cost, at a time when a conscious decision to buy might not be made.

Here's an example of how it works. If you invest $100 per month though a PAC, and the fund units are trading at $10 each on the day you buy, then you get ten shares on that date. If the price increased to $11 per unit the following month, then you would only purchase 9.1 units on that purchase day.

On the other hand, if the fund unit value declined to $9, then your $100 would buy 11.11 units on that purchase date, thus lowering your average cost.

Let the government make your RRSP contributions for you

If you have determined that the RRSP is your vehicle of choice, you can immediately increase your savings capacity by getting your tax refund back along the way. Arrange with your employer to withhold less income tax on each paycheque, by completing a CRA Form T1213. This is the *Request to Reduce Tax Deductions at Source for Year(s)* _____. It is available on the CRA website at *www.cra-arc.gc.ca*.

What is the advantage?

Let's say you have determined that you can free up $400 per month to invest. With a taxable income of $48,000, you decide that the immediate tax advantage of the RRSP and the long-term tax deferral on investment growth outweigh the disadvantage of having taxable withdrawals in retirement.

Contributing $4,800 to RRSP in that tax bracket should save you about $1,500 if you live in Ontario. If it comes as a lump sum refund next year, it can certainly be put to use. But what if you had access to it now, to increase your contribution and reduce your taxes even more?

If you complete a Form T1213 and have your monthly tax withholdings reduced by $125 and increase your RRSP contributions by this amount, then your total RRSP becomes $4,800 plus $1,500 or $6,300, and your projected tax savings increase to $1,900.

This is the amount that you can fill in on your T1213 and have the tax reduced by the higher amount.

In the long run, this strategy will increase your future RRSP by over 30%, compared to waiting until a tax refund is received and then spending it.

You can also use the form T1213 to decrease tax withholdings if you expect to have deductions for child care expenses, support payments, deductible employment expenses (where your conditions of employment require you to pay such expenses yourself), tax deductible interest on investment loans, investment counsel fees, large charitable donations or rental losses.

12

Freeing Up
Savings Capacity

TO REALLY GET YOUR PLAN WORKING, you will likely have to make some choices. To make informed choices, you need information.

Right now, do you know where all of your money goes? Do you know how you spend all of your money now?

That's step one.

Start with the deductions from your paycheque. Look at your gross pay and your net cheque amount, and make note of the difference between the two figures.

Write down how much goes to your Canada Pension Plan contribution, your Employment Insurance premium and to income taxes. How much goes to group insurance?

Does a portion go to any form of savings or retirement plan, including pension?

Are there any other deductions, like union dues or company social committee?

I hope you're writing all this down. As I've said before, writing things down—especially your goals and vision—embeds them in your brain much more effectively than typing them into a computer or tapping onto a tablet.

But using software like Quicken, Mint or Yodlee can be extremely powerful and help you produce reports and results analysis at the push of the finger. Over the medium and long term, you can identify trends and focus on areas for improvement. If you have access to the equipment necessary, these are incredibly valuable tools.

I love the ability to measure your progress, in ways like reducing debt, growing investments and overall net worth growth.

Back to counting your beans, and where your money goes, continue with that same exercise for all of your current spending. Find out where your money *really* goes, and let that information sink in. Make sure you account for all of your cash and loose change spending, including everything on credit or debit card, and all of your little cash withdrawals from the ATM.

Now, think about your short-term goals and your long-term vision. Get those planted in your mind and use your winner's mindset to commit to those goals.

Which of those expenses can you live without? Think back to what is most important to you, and decide which of those expenditures move you toward your goals, and which ones move you away.

Take advantage of windfalls

From time to time, you may come into a lump sum of money. It might be an income tax refund, a bonus at work, a gift from parents or an inheritance.

For many people, their tax refund is the biggest lump sum of tax-free cash they receive all year. And every year at tax time, I will happily give you a lecture about:
1. Putting that tax refund to use to address your highest priority goal; and,
2. Reducing your income tax withholdings at source, so that next year you can get that money working for you sooner, by getting the refund throughout the year.

A tax refund is not "free" money. It is money that you have **loaned to the government interest-free** for the time they have it.

If you receive a significant tax refund each year when you file, this means the income tax withholdings are too high on your regular paycheques. We have talked about the CRA form T1213 to apply for the required permission to reduce the withholdings. This is the optimal approach, by keeping the money on your side of the table and investing it immediately.

However, for some people, the opposite approach works better. In their case, planning for a refund is the only way they can put together a reasonably sized chunk of cash. If that's the case for you, then carry on with whatever is creating your refund, but let's make sure that cheque from CRA gets put to maximum use.

Remember those dreams you wrote down. How can you make best use of your refund to execute your plan? That may be the biggest lump sum of cash you come across all year.

It might be taking a big step toward paying off your credit card balance, that non-deductible line of credit, the allowable lump sum extra payment on your mortgage, an RRSP contribution, a TFSA deposit or Registered Education Savings Plan (RESP) contribution. Get excited about those goals, and make sure the cash ends up moving you toward them.

On the other hand, if your approach is to adjust your paycheque withholdings in order to increase your monthly cash flow, then calculate the monthly savings amount you need to reach your highest priority goal and make sure that amount is invested every paycheque.

Ensure you go through the full financial planning process—look at your current situation and things like assets and liabilities, re-read your written goals, examine that "gap" for opportunities and challenges, review your alternative strategies and options, make a decision and implement it.

Then periodically review your progress, to make sure you stay on track.

What better way to celebrate a windfall, than reaching some important goals!

13

Riding the Growth on Growth Phenomenon

EINSTEIN ONCE SAID that man's greatest invention was compound interest. That's a fascinating observation, given the observer.

He was commenting on the tremendous power of compound interest, and the positive effect it can have on so many lives. (As you know, if you have ever owed money at a high interest rate, compound interest working against you can also have a hugely negative effect.)

When you first invest, you are only earning interest or growth on your initial capital—the original money you invest. The magic of compound interest—or compound growth—is that over time, the growth is multiplied by growth on the growth, as well as on the original capital.

There is also an interesting mathematical phenomenon. There is a certain time period over which your money will double at any given growth rate, and then it will double again over the next similar period, and so on. The real power is in the fact that the end of the second double is really four times your original investment, and the third double is eight times, and the fourth one is 16 times.

You guessed it—the real magic and power is in starting early and then combining that with earning a high growth rate.

This compounding power is illustrated in something called the **Rule of 72**. Your rate of return divided into 72 gives you the number of years needed for each compounding period—the number of years it takes for your money to double. So, if your money is earning 5%, it takes 14.4 years to double. In 28.8 years, it will have grown to be four times its original amount.

At that rate of return, a $10,000 original investment becomes $20,000 in 14.4 years, and $40,000 in less than 29 years.

What if you can earn 10%? This reduces the doubling period down to 7.2 years, so $10,000 becomes $20,000 in 7.2 years, and in 14.4 years, it has become $40,000. MUCH more exciting is the fact that it will become $80,000 in 21.6 years, and $160,000 in less than 29 years! How long was it until your retirement...?

Realistically, though, we might be starting with small initial investments. Here is what happens over time to $100 invested once, at either 5% or 10%:

$100 One-time Investment

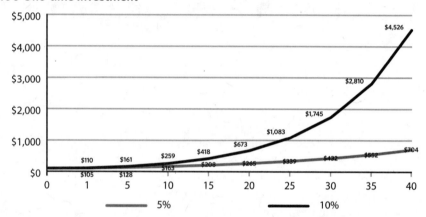

Can you believe that $100 can become $4,526 within a person's working career? Now, what if that person keeps investing, and puts away just $100 per month for that entire career? Here is the long-term effect of that, at average compound growth rates of 5% and 10%:

$100 Invested Per Month

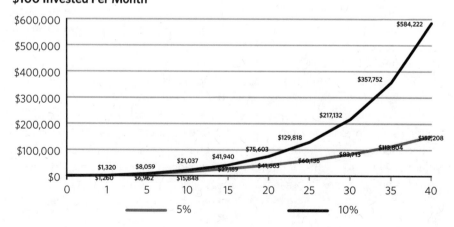

Even at a 5% average rate of return, foregoing a daily trip to Tim Horton's can become a significant portion of your retirement capital. At 10%, you can even start late, and produce a very comfortable retirement nest egg.

The secret? **Start now!**

14

Be an Owner, Not a Loaner

SO HOW DO YOU EARN 10% in a world where banks and governments are not even paying you 3% to borrow your money?

As we write this, banks are advertising "GIC rate specials" at 1% to 2.5%, locking in the money for one year to five years. "Virtual" and online institutions stretch this to 2.75%. Government bonds are even lower, unless you go for a much longer term.

When you invest in these instruments, you *loan* your money to the institution, which then turns around and loans your money to someone else at a higher interest rate, or invests the money in the shares of other companies, to earn more for the lending institution.

The banks do very well re-employing your capital for their profit, as you know. In the current climate, *you* don't do so well.

All great fortunes in history were created by owning a business. Whether you think of Bill Gates, Warren Buffett, the owners of Google and countless other

NO BULL

All great fortunes in history were created by owning a business.

Internet companies, or go back to the great fortunes of Carnegie, Guggenheim or J.P. Morgan, all of these fortunes have been built by owning companies.

Let's take it back to a more realistic and achievable level. In your city or town, most of the local fortunes have been made by people who own their own businesses. Likely the largest have been from "basic" industries like manufacturing, construction or even car sales. The lawyers and accountants are usually working for the business owners. Eventually, many business owners develop experienced staff who can take over the day-to-day running of the business, giving them more leisure time, or the ability to acquire or build up other businesses, if they are "serial entrepreneurs."

Here is my pitch for being a business owner, at some level, rather than only an employee. Take the example of highly paid professionals. Yes, many lawyers, chartered accountants and doctors do very well, but unless they own or partner in their businesses, and leverage the work of employees, they will only be building wealth by saving and investing a portion of what they earn, just like any other highly paid employee. Those that have built up significant wealth also usually own their own businesses.

In fact, most professional practices still require the personal toil of the professional in order to keep them profitable. Most professionals only get paid when they work.

Professionals who fail to build up significant equity in their practice, by training employees and developing a business that will run without them, have very little to sell when they retire.

In that situation, they have a job, but not a business.

I point out that difference, because fortunately *you* can invest in businesses where you do not have to show up for work every day. You can invest in businesses that are well run, have a proven track record of success and profitability, have a measurable past growth rate, and have a statutory requirement to regularly provide their investors—you, the owner—with their best guess as to what they expect to achieve in the future.

These are the publicly traded companies whose shares can be purchased on any business day, on the world's stock markets.

An added bonus to investing in these companies is that the owners can sell their shares on any business day, perhaps because their situation has changed or their outlook on the attractiveness of the company has diminished, or simply to lock in and enjoy a profit when the price is high.

Owning and operating your own business directly does not have that luxury of daily liquidity.

In the pages ahead, we detail many more of the pros and cons of investing in the shares of publicly traded companies, including the risks and tax advantages. The important concept for this chapter is that **you must become an owner if you**

expect to generate a rate of return in excess of inflation, and have a hope of achieving financial independence on your timeline.

Being a loaner means providing capital to other business people, who will use that capital to make more money. While loaning money—to governments or corporations, by investing in fixed income investments—will still have an important place in your investment portfolio, you will have to be an owner, with the risks and uncertainties that involves, in order to get ahead.

Being exclusively a loaner will simply not cut it.

NO BULL

You must become an owner if you expect to generate a rate of return in excess of inflation, and have a hope of achieving financial independence on your timeline.

15

Sharpening Your Horns

MY NEWSPAPER COLUMN READERS write me regularly for financial planning help. One recent email asked whether the writer should pay down her mortgage first or make an RRSP contribution. Another asked if he should be saving money for his child's education, or making RRSP contributions.

Still another was attempting to determine her optimal asset mix, realizing she is more risk-averse now than before the last stock market correction, but still wanting to take advantage of the long-term growth prospects for equities.

No matter what the specific issue or question, I found that there was commonality in the answers I gave—first, review your goals, and think of which choice will move you toward your priorities and your long-term vision. Then, we can talk about tactics and techniques, with confidence that you are asking the right questions and seeking the right answers.

Remember we have talked about **SMART goals**—specific, measurable, achievable, realistic and time-bound. A goal may start out with statements like, "I wish I did not owe so much money" or "I am so tired of making monthly payments and feeling like I am getting nowhere."

The **SMART goal statement** might be, "I will be completely out of debt other than my mortgage 24 months from now."

That can lead to an actionable plan. If the debts total $24,000, then the principal payments must be $1,000 per month, plus whatever interest charges apply. Is it possible to free up $1,000 per month from your spending plan? (Some people call this a "budget," but don't let that word scare you.)

If not, are there any options and alternatives to reach your goals faster or more efficiently?

Let's look at the options with debt elimination. If several debts, especially credit cards, can be consolidated into a loan at a lower interest rate, this will decrease the interest costs. That's one idea.

Perhaps you have low interest savings bonds or other savings accounts or deposits that are earning almost nothing, which would be better used to pay down high interest, non-deductible debt. Ultimately, you may have to decrease spending in order to free up the extra cash flow. If eliminating debt is your high-priority immediate goal, then that's the choice to make.

In all cases, look at your options, make decisions and start the action plan. Add in measureable milestones along the way. It is very important to measure progress. Progress is reinforcing, and regular measurement alerts us to any necessary adjustments to the plan as we go.

If the goal in question is a savings or investment objective, or another long-term target like retiring early, use the same process. It becomes even more important to have measurement milestones along the way for long-term goals.

Decide what really counts for you, and then get specific about what is needed to reach your goals.

If financial independence at 55 is your overriding objective, make that into a specific, measurable goal. Try to estimate how much annual income you will need from investments and other sources at that time.

What are your options to provide this future income? Will all of it come from your investments and properties initially, or will you develop a business that can ultimately be run by other people and provide you with income?

Decide on your chosen options. This is the basis of your plan, though the options can (and will) certainly evolve over time. But make a decision now, and get started.

Now, what do you have to do every month to make that plan happen?

Using a conservative estimate for rate of return for your chosen investment vehicles and allowing for inflation, determine how much you have to save each month. Can you afford it? If not, decide how much you can do now and commit to it.

Now, *the action plan*... in all cases, the single most important thing after writing down your goal is to start implementing your plan. I don't care if the plan is half-baked, imperfect or possibly inefficient—just start! You can always refine the plan as you go along, assuming you have not committed to some unchangeable product. Even the best, most perfect plan is going to need adjusting over time.

Don't dither; start now.

16

The Six-Step Financial Planning Process

AT THIS POINT, it should be clear that financial planning is an ongoing *process*, not a one-time event.

There are really six discrete steps involved in the process of creating the financial future you need. This process is a great framework for your overall planning, but it can also be applied to each separate financial issue and decision with which you are faced. Think of it as a decision-making process with which to approach any pressing problem.

And remember that research has proven that **the most important factor in achieving success is having specific goals and a written plan to reach those goals.** You can use the Six-Step Financial Planning Process[9] in the same way financial planning professionals use it to develop financial plans for clients.

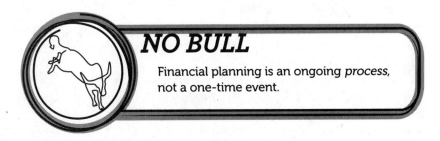

NO BULL

Financial planning is an ongoing *process*, not a one-time event.

---

[9] The Six-Step Process was originally developed by the Canadian Association of Financial Planners, and is now followed by successor professional organizations like the IAFP, Advocis and the CIFPS.

Step 1—A current snapshot

Step 1 is to determine your starting point. Where are you today? This applies in a number of areas, including income and expenses, assets and liabilities, investment values, current portfolio asset mix, and estate valuation in the event of death.

To determine your **net worth**, add up your assets (things you own) and your liabilities (amounts that you owe) and calculate the difference.

When you have an accurate Statement of Assets and Liabilities, you can set goals specific to growing assets and/or decreasing liabilities or tied to measuring your increase in net worth.

Cash flow—compare your current expenditures to your income. This helps you determine your saving capacity and the resources you have available to reach your bigger goals. You might want to set specific targets to decrease spending and live within your means. (Hey ... that's actually a very good idea!)

Estate planning and risk management are both important areas. If there are people who are financially dependent upon you, then the most critical thing to look at is what would happen if you died. Would your family have enough income? Do you know how much tax would be payable by your estate, and how much capital would be left over to replace your income?

Do you have a valid Will in place, to determine who would get your assets if you died?

What would happen if you became disabled?

Assess your life insurance needs and coverage, and income sources and needs in the event of disability. (Disability is several times more likely to occur than death during your working career.)

In the broader risk categories, what is your current insurance coverage on your property, and against liability claims?

All of the facts about your current situation are fair game for Step 1.

Step 2—Setting specific goals

Step 2 of the financial planning process is setting those specific, measurable goals that we've talked so much about. This is a statement of where you want to go, and how you want your life to be lived.

Start by sitting quietly and visualizing yourself six months, one year and three years from now. What does your ideal future look like? How good do you feel in this picture, after having achieved those goals?

Get specific. If your goal is "increase my net worth 10% by next December 31" then measure your net worth today, so you can put a specific dollar number on that goal and develop an actionable plan to reach it. Use your SMART Goal Worksheet to get really precise and measurable.

Step 3—What has to happen to get there?

Step 3 is determining the gap between where you are and where you want to go. This analysis will likely present both challenges and opportunities.

If your goal is to pay off certain debts by year end, then writing down all your specific obligations, their interest rates and payment amounts will show you opportunities to reduce the interest rate on some, and the advantages to focusing on certain debts first. By fixating on your goal, a plan will begin to develop.

Longer-term goals, like retiring at a certain age, with a certain amount of income in today's purchasing power, may require assistance from financial planning software or from a financial planner.

Don't hesitate to ask for help—I do.

Step 4—Options and alternatives

Step 4 is examining the alternate routes to your destination, as we described in the previous chapter. Again, help may be valuable. There is usually a variety of alternatives in financial planning and it's important that you examine several before you make your decision.

The next several parts of this book will help you with these options in several areas.

Step 5—Let's take action!

Step 5 is putting the ideas into action—executing your plan. Without action, there are only noble thoughts. Consistently implementing your plan is what will get you where you want to go. So get going.

Motivation will come from the excitement of the plan itself and the vision of success that it shows you. Reminding yourself throughout the year of your goals and your reasons for wanting to achieve them should be enough to keep you going through the tough times, which will crop up and try to deter you.

Step 6—The most important step for the rest of your life

Step 6 is to *regularly review your progress and update your plan as needed*. This is an important and ongoing activity to ensure that planning is a process rather than a one-time event. As your situation changes, your plan will need to be updated and modified.

For best success, this complete review and update should take place at least once a year, with quarterly measurements of progress along the way. If you are inclined to do it monthly, that's even better.

Financial planning may not be an exciting sport, but achieving financial success is. It is the foundation for freedom in the rest of your life. Tackle it now!

NO BULL

As your situation changes, your plan will need to be updated and modified.

17

Assembling Your Team

DO YOU NEED a financial planner or advisor?

Not everyone needs a financial advisor to achieve financial success. Many people have done very well researching, planning, saving and investing on their own.

After all, you are presumably the person who cares most about reaching your financial goals, and therefore you are the one who is most invested in your own success. You are the one who has to make the choices. **You are the most important person on the team.**

Having said that, many people do much better with the assistance of a financial planner or advisor. A good planner will help in the development of your initial financial plan, making your goals specific, calculating the resources needed to reach them, helping to set priorities and make choices, and then in the implementation of the plan. Often, that last step is critical.

A *great* planner or advisor will help you monitor your plan, provide annual updates and adjustments, recommend mid-course corrections and, generally, make sure things happen.

One of my mentors, Doug Macdonald, R.F.P., always said that a financial plan was a little like aiming a rifle at a distant target—minor adjustments now can make huge differences 10 or 20 years out, and often the difference between hitting a bull's eye and missing the target completely.

He also said that the initial plan was simply the first step on the journey. The most important determinant of long term success was the regular review of progress, the adjustments for changing circumstances, and the wise choices made over the years and the decades. (I guess that's one reason we have such long term relationships with our clients.)

A good advisor will get to know your situation, and be there with appropriate advice when needed, as life events challenge you and reward you.

Scientific research studies have proven that people with advisors accumulate more assets than those without, by margins as wide as four times. A Canadian study repeated over four consecutive years with over 1,000 investors found that advisors provided "... durable values that benefit their clients throughout their investing lifetimes, such as the early adoption of a savings and investment culture, the avoidance of common behavioral investment errors, and the value of developing and following a financial plan."[10]

Advisors can help sort through financial products and options, develop tax effective investment plans and appropriate asset mix.

For many people, the value of the advice can be significant.

On the other hand, you might be one of those people who will achieve greater success doing it on your own. A 2009 study in Germany called "Do financial advisors improve performance?" found that some financial advisors lower the returns and increase the risk profile of their client portfolios.[11] (Interestingly, the same study also showed that investors who delegate the portfolio management achieve better results, but the researchers attributed this to the fact that advisors tend to be managing richer, older investors.)

Your task is to decide if you are one of those people who can benefit from the services of a good financial planner or advisor and, if so, figure out where to find one and how to develop a mutually rewarding relationship.

One important caution—some "advisory" relationships may be detrimental to your financial health.

While I strongly believe that a positive, appropriate advisory relationship can allow you to achieve your goals years sooner than working on your own, not all advisory relationships have those characteristics.

A *good* advisor—who specializes in the areas appropriate for your needs, who will provide you with the time required to provide the right plan, products and prodding you need—can be almost as important to your long term success as having the right life partner can be to your overall happiness.

You may be able to do all of this on your own, but most people do better with a coach, and ideally that coach is an expert in the field. So, finding that relationship for you—the advisory one, that is—has to be our goal.

---

[10] IFIC, *Value of Advice Report, 2010 and 2011*, The Investment Funds Institute of Canada.

[11] Andres Hackethal, Haliassos Michalis, and Tulio Jappelli; *Do financial advisors improve performance?;* VOX, (2009).

Remember I said that I have several financial advisors as clients? They appreciate the value of a second set of eyes, a different perspective, and an advisor who specializes in their issues and concerns. Not all of them are actually experts in the areas they personally need, as they may have developed other specialties based on market needs, like only assisting retired people, for example. Other times, they just get tremendous value from someone—in this case, me—who asks the right questions, who challenges some of their beliefs and helps them improve the quality of their decision making.

So, if I'm a big proponent of your seeking and achieving a positive advisory relationship, why do I say the wrong relationship can be detrimental?

In many cases, a relationship might simply be not appropriate—a bad fit between the client and advisor—where the advisor or financial institution doesn't specialize in the areas of advice that the client needs at a particular stage in life or stage of their financial plan.

Examples of unsuitability would be trying to work with an advisory team that only services retired people or high net worth individuals, when you are a young person starting out and needing financial education, real financial planning help and savings strategies. The advisor's exclusive specialty and focus might be structuring investment portfolios of $1 million or more and helping older people with retirement income strategies.

They might also only provide their "A" level service to people from whom they collect $10,000 or more per year in fees, which you have no hope of providing. Ask those questions.

Most real financial planners, financial advisors or investment advisors will tell you right away whether or not your situation fits their specialty and service model, but unfortunately some won't. Some advisors will accept any clients, and then set about trying to figure out how to generate revenue from them. This can result in the negatives to which I referred above.

These advisors might be well-intentioned but poorly trained, or they might even be unscrupulous or simply bad business people. Either way, the negative results can include purchasing expensive, inappropriate insurance or investment products. Best case is those products will be needed at some point, but were simply not your current priority. Worst case is that they are not necessary, or they are bad products or strategies that will actually set you back on your plan.

So, how do you know? How do you find and select an advisor who will be a key member of your team and a positive force in helping you achieve your goals?

Before tackling these questions, I need you to keep in mind that the terms "financial consultant," "financial advisor," "investment advisor," and even "financial planner" have no meaning in law or in regulations. These are like the terms "bookkeeper" or "accountant."

You can call yourself an accountant or a financial planner, and no one can stop you, except in Quebec, where the terms "financial planner" and "planificateur financier" are regulated, and the practice of financial planning is regulated.

The lack of regulation means you need to search out professional planning designations, such as "Registered Financial Planner" (R.F.P.®) or "Certified Financial Planner" (CFP®). These are designations or licenses issued by financial planning practitioner organizations. The designations show evidence of education, experience and commitment to abide by a published code of ethics and written practice standards.

A financial planning designation or approach is NOT required in order to be licensed to sell investment products. So-called investment advisors are actually licensed as "Registered Representative," "Investment Salesperson," "Mutual Fund Representative" or similar titles, and registered with provincial securities commissions, and then regulated in their investment roles either by IIROC or MFDA.

IIROC is the Investment Industry Regulatory Organization of Canada, the self-regulatory organization of investment dealers and their employees.

The Mutual Fund Dealers Association (MFDA) self-regulates mutual fund dealers, as you no doubt figured out. Both of these organizations have regulatory authority delegated to them by the provincial securities commissions, and are responsible for setting rules for investment salespeople and advisors, and disciplining those who transgress.

The provincial securities commissions directly regulate the Portfolio Manager profession.

For a listing of professional designations and other information, go to websites operated by the Ontario Securities Commission or your provincial securities commission.

See our appendix for a full listing of all of the organizations involved.

18

What to Look for in an Advisory Relationship

I THINK OFTEN ABOUT what constitutes value in a business relationship. This is an ongoing obsession with me, and I have had some insights over the years that may help you.

One of our activities has always been to ferret out the most appropriate investment suppliers and products, and to negotiate reduced commissions and fees on the clients' behalf. As independent fee-for-service advisors, paid ONLY by our clients, we divorced ourselves from the compensation paid by the products and suppliers, so we could focus on providing the best value for our clients. Not all advisors have that luxury.

Clearly, if we can reduce the costs and overhead of investing, then we have provided value for the client, compared to them using the same products at higher costs. Simple.

The *real value*, though, is discriminating between a commodity—which you can get anywhere so you shop on price—and a unique or value-added service, where a higher price is justified.

In our discussions with suppliers, I sometimes notice that I have a philosophy not totally shared by all investment product providers. I have this belief, which becomes more entrenched as I get older, that every client is different.

Every person I meet has a different situation than the last. There are differences in their hopes and dreams and fears. There are differences in the dangers they must face, overcome and protect against. There are differences in the opportunities, resources and strengths they can leverage to achieve their goals. There are differences in their comfort level and preferred approach. They are each unique.

Paradoxically, this philosophy has caused me guilt as a business owner. "Guilt" is an odd word to use in this context, but it is the word that fits. Over the years, I have read a number of business books and listened to gurus who espouse standardization and mass production as a means to make a business more efficient, which means more profitable. They suggest that a business provide the same service or product to everyone and try to convince them that it fits their situation.

I come across variations of this approach with investment product providers and "advisors," although many are sophisticated enough to have what they call "mass customization." This means that everyone uses the same product, but some aspect of it is customized so that they can say it is "personalized."

My misplaced guilt is that, as a business owner, I have not forced our company into this type of standardization, which the business books tell me will produce greater profit for our shareholders, our employees, and my family.

Here's where it gets a little tricky for consumers of financial products and advice. **Which approach constitutes value in your unique situation?**

If you are fully informed about your needs—and about the options available to you—then a standardized product might work fine, for at least a portion of your situation. If you are confident about that, the next step is to make sure that you are getting it at a good price.

If you're paying a premium price, then make sure you're getting a premium service.

Obviously, the ideal is to find a premium service at a less than premium price. You usually have to have some negotiating power to achieve that.

My advice is to try to find out as much as you can about the service or product being offered, the real costs, and whether or not this same product can be obtained elsewhere at a lower price.

Is it a commodity? Then shop on price.

On the other hand, is there personalized value being added that is relevant to your situation? If that's the case, a higher (but still reasonable) price probably represents good value, and is probably the best choice. (A fool is a man who knows the price of everything and the value of nothing.)

An advisor or financial planner who spends time with you to really understand your uniqueness, and who asks detailed questions about your situation, and what you want to achieve, should be paid more than one who just says, "Oh, you're 30 and make $40,000. Here's what you need."

The customized approach is much more likely to result in an appropriate plan that will speed you toward your goals. Any payment to that advisor will be money well spent. The other approach is more likely to make money for the advisor, even if they appear to be charging you less.

By the way, I finally overcame my guilt by reading a book called *The Strategic Enterprise* by Bill Bishop. It's a must-read for any business owner or general manager. Bishop's thesis is that old-style businesses are based on the Product-First Formula, while successful businesses of the future are based on the Relationship-First Formula. These enterprises design their business around the needs of customers (not products), and focus on providing value based on customers' unique needs.

"Eventually, every order will be a custom order."[12] Eureka! Somebody thinks we're doing it right.

When Bishop made that prediction in 2000, it seemed far-fetched, but technology has brought it to virtually every doorstep. Another quote particularly hit home with me: "No matter what customers want, the Strategic Enterprise is dedicated to helping them get it. If the customer wants the competitor's product, the Strategic Enterprise helps him get it."

This type of company—and financial advisor—doesn't fear competition, because it acts as a conduit to the competition, if they have a more appropriate product or service for that customer. This type of company doesn't fear the fact that today's consumers are informed and empowered, and in fact devotes itself to educating, informing and empowering the consumer even more.

When you are shopping for financial services and advice, keep this ideal in mind, and seek out enterprises that can deliver to you.

---

[12] Bill Bishop, *The Strategic Enterprise: Growing a Business for the 21st Century.* Stoddart (2000).

19

How to Get the Most Value from Your Advisor

ONE WAY OR ANOTHER, you likely pay something for financial advice. All but the most ardent do-it-yourselfer uses a financial product or service that has a cost attached to it.

In a perfect world, these costs would be "unbundled" for you, showing you exactly how much you are paying for each of:

- advice,
- investment management services,
- administration and reporting,
- and other costs, if any.

Unbundling and transparency is becoming more common and this is the future of the financial services industry. However, in reality, these costs are still often bundled together.

No matter what your arrangement, though, we assume that you want to get the best possible value from your advisory relationship. This means actually establishing such a relationship with an individual advisor, as a first step, as opposed to simply purchasing products over the counter at a bank or credit union, or over the internet.

At our office, we muse from time to time about why some clients have a great relationship with us and get a tremendous amount of value from what we provide, while others make it more challenging for us to provide them with true value.

Rather than reveal all of my own secrets, I have looked to Dan Richards, president of a firm called Strategic Imperatives, to provide some suggestions.

Dan has been an observer, coach, commentator and even CEO in the financial industry. Some years ago, he hosted a series of luncheons with successful financial advisors and talked to them about the clients with whom those advisors had the strongest and most successful relationships.

Here is what those advisors revealed, interspersed with my own opinions and editorial comments.

Be honest

Being honest means fully disclosing relevant information to your advisors, so they can provide you with top quality advice. If I don't tell my doctor everything relevant, I can't expect a precise diagnosis or accurate prescription.

Honesty also means responding candidly when an advisor makes a recommendation or asks your opinion about the style or usefulness of her advice and services. Don't just nod and say "everything's okay," the way most of us do at a restaurant. If they are falling short, let them know it, and be prepared to be as clear as you can about what else you need from them.

Honesty also means being candid and working toward developing a common, compelling vision for your future. The clearer your advisor's picture of your desired future, the better your chance of achieving it.

Invest time up front

We provide our new clients with an abundance of homework so that we can really get to know them, before we start to provide advice. We are fixated on finding out a person's most important goals and objectives, so that all recommendations help move them toward fulfillment of those dreams.

Spend the time to get your message across fully and accurately. If the advisor gives you questionnaires to fill out, do them as completely as you can. Even go further—if all you are given is the standard "KYC" form to complete (Know Your Client) with very basic questions about income, employer and net worth, demand an interview where you are asked about your real goals, priorities, fears and service requirements.

Continue to commit regular time

Try to respond to your advisor quickly and completely, whenever additional information is needed. If forms need to be signed, get together or return the information on a timely basis. Delays or no response from clients is the cause of 90% of the mistakes that we see—clients fail to return information or forms promptly, and subsequently risk missing deadlines or opportunities.

Advisors are under tremendous pressure these days from regulators, compliance departments and the demands of paperwork. Even if some of this paperwork seems unreasonable, help out as best you can.

Be consistent

Most changes to your plan, strategy, risk tolerance and other factors should be gradual and evolutionary, not 180 degrees. Obviously, the exception is when there is a life event that occurs, like a change or loss of job, marriage, birth of a child or death in the family. Inform your advisor immediately about any such events.

However, the message here is to be clear on who you are and try to be consistent with your requests and your approach. For example, don't switch overnight from being a growth-oriented investor to an income-oriented investor, every time the market goes up or down.

Try to maintain perspective

Money can be a very emotional thing, especially when the stock markets are collapsing. The stress can be magnified by inflammatory media headlines.

As an investor and client, try to maintain an even keel, as opposed to over-reacting to all of the fact and fiction in the media. Keep in mind that the more you watch business or investment news, the more you will hear conflicting points of view and the more you will be subjected to added stress.

Try to walk the fine line of staying informed, but not feeling you must react to everything you hear or read.

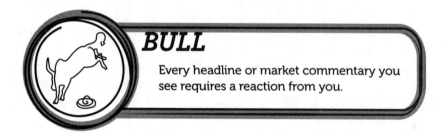

BULL

Every headline or market commentary you see requires a reaction from you.

Be open-minded

If you are always cynical or distrustful of the advice your advisor gives you, it's time for a new advisor. You always need to ask all of your questions, and even have a healthy dose of skepticism, but hear the arguments and recommendations first, before closing your mind.

This may be the crux of the relationship. If you trust enough to listen, learn and try out suggestions that make sense, you have the basis of a good relationship. If you always need a second opinion, and your initial reaction is, "I think he's full of $&%*," then it's likely time to move on.

Be reasonable

Reasonableness shows up in expectations of performance, and about the knowledge and expertise your advisor is expected to possess in areas outside his or her specialty.

Also be reasonable in your expectations of service level, based on the amounts of fees you are actually paying to the advisor. I have met many clients over the years whose advisor's share of their management fees are only a few hundred dollars a year, yet they expect the kind of service they get at the Lexus dealer, where they might have provided a profit of $20,000 when they bought their car.

Finally, some good advice from another Dan, this one Dan Sullivan, founder of The Strategic Coach program. His basic rules for advisors—which apply equally to clients—are:

1. Do what you say you are going to do;
2. Show up on time;
3. Say please and thank you.
   I wish I had said that.

Managing the Bull:
Detect and Deflect the Crap

WE HAD DEFINED the over arching goal of long-term financial planning as achieving the point where your wealth, rather than your work, will support your lifestyle and goals.

Reaching that summit is all about accumulating capital through savings and compound growth, and then converting that capital into steady, reliable income. Learning the techniques for both is very important at each stage.

The framework for your planning is based on the Six-Step Financial Planning Process. The steps are:

1. Take a snapshot of where you are today.
2. Become clear and specific on where you want to go.
3. Calculate what is needed to get from here to there.
4. Examine alternative methods and decide on the optimal for each goal.
5. Implement the decisions in the plan, and
6. Periodically update and adjust the plan.

Most people will spend the first third or half of their financial planning life accumulating capital through savings and making it grow through investing. The fundamental concept to achieving success in this endeavor is to pay yourself first, and make sure that money from every single paycheque goes to work your short and long-term financial goals.

You are the most important person on your financial planning team, and you are the one most invested in achieving your financial success. Many consumers also benefit from the advice of a good financial planner or financial advisor, although many people also do well on their own.

By carefully selecting an appropriate advisor, asking a lot of questions up front and being open and candid about your own goals, needs and expectations, you can establish and maintain a mutually valuable relationship with an advisor. If you achieve that, your chances of success rise significantly.

Maintaining a great financial advisory relationship means practicing many of the same qualities required to grow any relationship. These include honesty, consistency, responsiveness and openness.

The journey can be shorter with the right team assembled.

Part 3

Tightening the Reins: Earning and Spending Wisely

"It's not what you make; it's what you keep."

\- JOHN CHRISTIANSON
(GREAT CANADIAN)

20

What's Your Vision for Your "Life Arc"?

DAN AND RITA got married in their mid-twenties. Rita had just started her first full-time career job and Dan was in his last semester at university. With Rita's income and some wedding gifts, they were able to move from an apartment to a rental house and buy a sketchy amount of furniture.

The place looked pretty bare for a couple of years, but their lifestyle was not what you would call simple. They kept very active with outdoor sports, walking, hiking, cross-country skiing and the like, but managed to stay away from the club scene. They loved entertaining at home, so they started to make their own wine in the basement.

Since they did not own a TV (and saved on cable), an indulgence was heading to the Cineplex for a movie on the big screen, on deal night. They watched several high-quality TV series on their laptops, and debated a Netflix subscription. At eight dollars per month, they realized that could save them a lot of money going to the movies.

When Dan started working full-time as an executive trainee at a manufacturing company, they suddenly had surplus income. He used his first few paycheques to purchase some much-needed furniture and appliances, and then they decided they really wanted ("and deserved!") a winter vacation and some serious indulgences, after five years of school and living very frugally.

Here is where they really started to make some very smart choices, choices that paid off for the rest of their lives. They had that sense that some people have, of where they wanted their lives to go, and which choices would take them there. They had that vision of the Life Arc they wanted to create for themselves.

Many people in their position would use their credit cards to start buying all the things they wanted, assuming they will pay off the credit card balance with their future higher incomes. The problem is that once the door is open, it seldom gets closed. What almost always happens is that people quite innocently go too far and end up with a balance they can't pay off by the due date. The response is usually, "Hey, no problem, we can handle these payments and eliminate the balance within a couple of months."

Then the interest charges begin, and a few more "while we're at it" purchases start to kick in. Soon the good intention of paying the balance off completely in any given month has slid out the window.

In a perfect world, no one would have a credit card until he or she had enough surplus cash flow to pay it off comfortably each month. Then they could happily use the bank's money free for up to 21 days each month, and cash in on the various incentives that credit card companies provide so we choose them over their competitors. (More on that scam later.)

But, realistically, we all need a credit card in today's world. Without it, you can't make online purchases, check into a hotel, rent a car or participate in many other activities in life. As well, proper use of a credit card is a big step toward establishing a good credit rating.

Back to Dan and Rita. Here are the great choices they made, while still getting everything they wanted.

They made a list of all the things they could possibly desire. They realized that buying their own house was high on the list, as was replacing their 12-year-old Nissan Sentra, despite its charming areas of rust. Unfortunately, Dan's new place of work was not serviced by public transit, though at least he had free parking there.

So the list got trimmed a little. Remaining was a two-week winter vacation in Cancun, replacing the car and saving for a down payment on a house.

They set up a savings account for each want, and decided how much to put away every paycheque toward each goal. They were lucky that they had not yet committed Dan's new income to any regular lifestyle obligations, loan payments, or other bad habits. After arranging a monthly contribution to RRSP and leaving $100 per month uncommitted for emergencies and surprises, this gave them $925 per paycheque to play with, which they assigned to the remaining goals.

Here's how their plan shook out, starting May 1:

1. $125 to a "decadence account," to blow in any manner they desired.
2. $325 to winter vacation, to have $5,000 ready by the end of January. In the meantime, they enjoyed weekly online shopping for the best deals, quickly realizing that they could save thousands if they became flexible about their destination and waited for a last-minute deal. They decided that any money left over would go towards a "new" car.

3. $300 to car fund, to have $4,000 ready by year-end. They had a friend who drove a fabulous used SUV that he got for $9,000, and bragged continually about how wonderful it was to have no monthly payments. While the market value of their Sentra appeared to only be about $3,000, they thought selling it and adding the proceeds to their accumulated cash would give them a good start toward getting a newer, more reliable vehicle without a bank loan.
4. $175 toward a down payment on a house.

They quickly realized that they would never own a house at that rate. However, on reassessment, they still both wanted the winter vacation and really felt the car was needed. So they committed that, after the winter vacation and the car had been fully funded, they would move both of those monthly payments to the house account. Any future vacation funding would come from pay raises and voluntary recovery from the "decadence" fund.

Now, why do I say that Rita and Dan made choices that would positively affect the rest of their lives?

First, they sat down and made a list of everything they wanted, agreed upon the priorities, and put a plan in place to reach them. They were going to get everything they wanted and, knowing that, they were able to enjoy the anticipation of having those goals achieved, instead of having them indulged immediately, with the accompanying buyer's remorse and debt hangover.

Secondly—and perhaps most important—they have put in place a rewarding and self-fulfilling process of goal achievement and sound financial management, that would serve them through their entire lives. By learning this lesson early in a positive fashion, instead of learning it by having to dig out from the deep hole of debt, they saved themselves thousands of dollars of "tuition" and achieved a head start on their important goals.

Finally, they got what they wanted. Remember, that's the idea behind everything we say in this book. I want you to have it all, but "all" has to be defined in terms of your own resources and realistic timing.

I've been in the workforce for over 30 years, making an income that is above average, but I still have to make choices every day, because I can't afford everything. However, what I can tell you for sure is I have always regretted going into debt for indulgences or to purchase depreciating assets, and have always got a lot more satisfaction from saving up and paying cash.

Postscript—in September, Dan and Rita were hit with a $1,000 car repair bill. When they had to put that on their credit card and then "rob" their car fund to pay the credit card off, they realized they needed to have an emergency fund on hand. The uncommitted "extra money" had mysteriously disappeared. They agreed to set up a fourth account and divert their previous indulgence money and the uncommitted surplus into this, until it grew to $3,000. Dan agreed to give up his daily Starbucks latte, which incidentally saves them $1,140 per year, or about $80 per month from the indulgence fund.

Whatever your age, are there any lessons you can take from their experience?

21

Becoming Jedi Debt Master

THIS SECTION OF THE BOOK is devoted to making you a smarter consumer, borrower and money manager. Falling too deeply into debt has cost more Canadians their chance at financial independence than all other reasons combined.

There is unprecedented pressure these days to obtain and maintain a luxurious lifestyle and indulge in all the wonderful material things that today's society can offer. We used to call it keeping up with the Joneses.

I understand that. I'm subject to those pressures every day, as well.

The irony is that owing money, which was borrowed initially to finance a fancy lifestyle, becomes the main obstacle to maintaining that lifestyle.

The secret to having the **sustainable** lifestyle is to wait a very short time until you can pay for that lifestyle with cash. It is a subtle, but profound, change in attitude.

What I can tell you with absolute certainty is that such a change becomes self rewarding and even addictive. Waiting to purchase something lets you enjoy

NO BULL
The secret to having the **sustainable** lifestyle is to wait a very short time until you can pay for that lifestyle with cash.

the anticipation that much longer, and paying cash gives you the luxury of really enjoying it, without guilt or pressure to repay.

Surplus cash flow gives you the ability to choose your goals, to build equity faster and to enjoy the unique and wonderful feeling of having available cash.

Living within your means allows you to avoid the horrible feeling of wondering if you will make it to your next paycheque before running out of money, or to the end of the month on your available credit. It avoids calls from creditors. It avoids working for years to rebuild your credit rating, so you can build your wealth faster by using "good" debt.

You will almost certainly have to borrow money in your life, if for no other reason than to buy a house. That's why we are devoting a section of this book to the proper use of credit, with individual chapters on the two largest purchases you will probably ever make, a house and car.

We want you to win the credit game, and not be cannon fodder for the financial institutions. We want you to be one of the people who uses credit and borrowing to accelerate your wealth creation, and not have it sabotage your financial plan.

You may have to borrow money to buy a house, but you will never **have to** borrow money to purchase a television set or tropical vacation. Our goal here is to help you develop an ingrained mindset that will automatically prevent you from making any such mistakes.

Use your Winner's Mindset in all your dealings with financial institutions

There's a wonderful saying, "You don't get what you deserve in life; you get what you **negotiate**."

Always, always ask for a better interest rate than the financial institution is advertising, or than they first offer you. Ask them to waive set up or appraisal fees. Ask for anything else you think is reasonable.

Be polite, but be firm. A strong negotiating position comes from talking to at least two institutions at any one time, and be honourable by letting them know that

NO BULL
Always use your Winner's Mindset to negotiate a better deal with financial institutions.

you are doing this. That's what competition is all about. Make sure they know that they need a sharp pencil to get your business.

When you negotiate on a large transaction like a mortgage, you may have even more leverage to make a better deal. Talk to a mortgage broker and search rates online, before talking to your own bank or credit union. Give them every chance to match the best rate you find, and let them know that you really want to continue your relationship with them, so you hope they can provide you with just as good a deal.

In the end, the best debt is probably no debt, but in Chapter 28 we talk about good debt and bad debt. Part of mastering the use of credit is to always think about using other people's money to make money, but using your own to pay for things that wear out or get used up.

Always read the fine print on offers and loan agreements. Here's why:

An electronics firm offers "no payments, no interest for 18 months." Sounds great, so you take the offer. Problem is, you end up being two days late in paying it off at the other end. It's easy to forget after 18 months.

What does the fine print say? The company had clearly stated that any late payments—or even paying 90% but not the entire loan off on time—resulted in a whopping 24% interest per year applied retroactively.

Zero interest deals work the same way. Any balance—*even $10*—left at the end of the term means retroactive interest to day one, at rates that would make American bankers blush.

Some agreements add administrative and collection costs on top of that interest.

You can certainly take advantage of great offers, but be very clear on your obligations, and the potential penalties hanging over your head.

Even with bank loans and mortgages, read through the documents before signing. You may be surprised by things like the way interest is calculated and charged, or by the fact that with an "unsecured" loan the bank could now have a claim on all of your assets, to satisfy your indebtedness.

Being smart about credit, negotiating better deals and only using debt to grow your wealth are guaranteed ways to move more quickly toward financial independence.

And I can now make a toast to your success, with a bottle of expensive wine that I waited years to purchase, and naturally paid for with cash!

22

Don't Get Trampled by Bad Choices on Banking and Credit

DO ME A FAVOUR. Pull out your last credit card bill. Look at where it says something like, "Reminder: If you only make the minimum payment every month, it will take approximately 56 years and one month to pay the entire balance shown on the statement."

That's a direct quote from my most recent monthly credit card statement.

Fifty-six freaking years!

And that assumes no new purchases or charges in any of those 56 years. What are the chances of that? The interest cost at 20% per year is enormous.

This is what the combination of high interest rate and low payments creates. (By the way, that combination is precisely the magic formula used in thousands of consumer ads promising you the luxury goods, electronics, furniture, cars, jewelry and clothing you want, at "affordable" monthly payments.)

Thank goodness, all credit card companies are now required to provide a disclosure on the repayment time period on each statement. The number of years will vary, as the minimum payment on larger balances is a smaller proportion

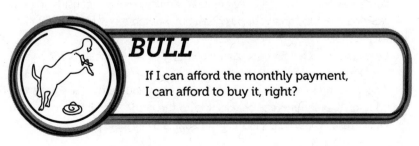

BULL

If I can afford the monthly payment, I can afford to buy it, right?

of the total than on small balances, thus resulting in a longer repayment period. Again, the lower your payment, the higher your total interest cost and the higher your total cost of borrowing.

While you've got your credit card statement handy, check out the area under interest rates. I was a little shocked to see that my last statement showed 19.99% interest on the regular purchases and 21.5% on cash advances.

Just for fun, I flipped it over and read the fine print on how they charge interest. This told me that failing to pay the balance in full in any given month meant interest would then be charged retroactively to the date of purchase for each transaction. That's why the failure to pay every credit card balance off completely and on time every month causes so much damage.

Banks didn't become Canada's most profitable institutions by being charitable to their customers. Huge profits are made by lending money to consumers. That's totally fair, if everyone knows and understands the rules and the ramifications of borrowing and paying interest costs. The problem is that the most naïve and vulnerable of us are the ones who end up in the most trouble.

A poor understanding of the proper uses of debt is a major reason why rich Canadians get wealthier, while the poor stay poor.

If you find yourself deep in credit card debt, you have to take action quickly. Luckily, it's a very competitive business with high costs for obtaining new customers. You can use that to your advantage.

Here are the immediate steps to take:

1. Identify at least $10 a day of spending that you can eliminate, and commit toward payments on your credit cards.
2. Read your statements to determine the exact interest rate you are currently paying.
3. Open the junk mail you receive with "pre-approved" credit card offers, read the ads and scour the internet for low interest rate cards and extended periods of interest holidays on balances that you transfer in.
4. Write down the details of your best offer, call the customer service number on your current credit card, and ask to talk to a supervisor. Don't talk to the person who answers the phone. Tell the supervisor which company is offering you a 4% rate with an interest holiday, and say you are considering transferring your balance and your business, but wanted to give them first chance to match the offer.
5. Be prepared to follow through, by completing an application for an alternate card and making the move.
6. Above all, make sure that that $10 a day—or double that, if you can identify additional expenditures—makes it onto the credit card balance each month, while the card itself stays safely (and unused) inside a drawer.

Ideally, reduce to just one card. This makes it easier for you to focus your attention and your extra payments, and has the added bonus of cutting down on paperwork.

Right now, take the first steps to taking charge of your debts.

Your biggest debt will be your mortgage

Whether you own a home now or dream of buying one in the future, it pays to understand the mortgage rules, and some of the easy ways to pay your mortgage off more quickly.

When you take out a mortgage on a 25-year amortization, do you know how much of your payment goes to interest in the first year?

It's about 97%. (It has been argued that you really go from renting a house to renting the money, though that ignores the fact that the increase in value of the house belongs to you.)

A $100,000 mortgage at 4.2% paid off over 25 years results in total interest costs of $61,000. So the $100,000 loan actually costs $161,000, even at a very reasonable interest rate. At an 8% interest rate, the interest cost jumps to $129,000 and the total cost to $229,000.

The first and easiest step is to accelerate your payments by matching them to your pay periods. If you get paid biweekly, that means you have 26 pay periods in a year. By paying half of your regular monthly mortgage payment on a biweekly basis, you make two extra payments per year, painlessly.

This alone will reduce a 25-year amortization mortgage to 21.7 years, and reduce the total interest cost in the example above to $51,900.

Increasing the payments slightly can knock off additional years, and is well worth your while. For the price of skipping a $4 trip to Tim Horton's or Starbucks daily, you can shorten that amortization to 15 years, and the total interest cost to $33,750.

Not only that, if you sell the house in five years to upgrade, you will have paid down over $27,000 of principal, building equity quickly on top of any market value increase. On the other hand, a 25-year amortization with monthly payments will

NO BULL

Skipping your daily coffee stop can save you seven years of mortgage payments, and $33,000 interest!

only reduce the principal by $11,000 in the first five years, leaving you holding $89,000 after five years of hard-earned payments.

In 2012, the federal government tightened up the rules for mortgages once again, reducing the maximum amortization from 30 years to 25 years.

Hallelujah! They did something right.

Although the change makes it slightly harder for people to own a house, anyone who needed the longer amortization at today's low interest rates in order to make a house purchase doable was playing Russian roulette. A one percent increase in interest rates would raise the monthly payments by quite a bit more than the decrease in amortization from 30 to 25 years.

For most people, their house is likely to be the biggest purchase they ever make. Remarkably, many of those homeowners have only a vague understanding of the time value of money, and how much they are really paying for their mortgage. Perhaps more tragically, many find out too late how easy it is to save tens of thousands of dollars over the term of the mortgage, and own the house free and clear decades earlier.

Every bank and credit union has a mortgage calculator on their websites. If you have a mortgage, or buying a house is in your dreams, get on one of those calculators and find out how easy it is to afford a house at today's rates. Then experiment to learn all the variables, and how simple it is to reduce your long-term interest costs.

Oh, yes—and I expect to be invited to your mortgage burning party!

23

Grab Your Debts
by the Reins

IT'S QUITE LIKELY that you came to this book owing money. If you are debt free other than your mortgage, that puts you in a very small minority of Canadians.

One way to improve your standard of living and have more money to spend is to reduce your debt service—the amount of money that goes out every month for payments on obligations.

Yes, this is easier said than done, but a systematic approach can allow you to get out from under and free up money for your personal wants and your savings for future needs.

Personal bankruptcies in Canada are at near record levels, marriages break down because of debt, and thousands of people fail to achieve their financial goals simply because of excessive borrowing. I won't spend a lot of time over-dramatizing the problem. If you're in the situation where you struggle from payday to payday, then you know how it feels.

If you're not, you likely know someone who is, and you may have been exposed to the kind of pressure they feel. Either way, it's not pretty.

Most people in that situation know they have a problem. Many seek help, but many don't know where to turn. I suggest a non-profit community credit counselling service, which is available in most large cities. There is a national association that can make referrals, at 1-866-398-5999 or email to contact@CreditCounsellingCanada.ca.

But what if your situation is more like Canada's, which is running an annual deficit but plans to balance its budget in three years, and enjoys respect from its lenders? How do you determine when debts have become a debt problem?

Clue number one is running an annual cash flow deficit, where your expenditures exceed your income. If some of those expenditures are debt servicing costs, then you have a debt problem.

And if you can't service all your debts at today's record low interest rates, then you will have a really serious problem when rates go up.

The first step is to take stock of where you are, and be brutally honest with yourself.

This may be painful, but list all of your debts. Rank them first by interest rate. You may have to read the fine print of your credit card agreement or call the company to find out for sure. Don't be shocked if you find that you're paying interest higher than 20% on some of them. Such outrageous rates are not unusual for retail chain charge cards.

If you have ever taken or considered a payday loan, realize that the interest rate on that little cash advance is likely as high as 59% per year.

Your first priority should be those high interest rate charge cards and other loans. These cost you the most money and are the most difficult to pay off. However, we assume you don't have the cash to pay these off or you would have. So what about refinancing?

Can you arrange a line of credit or term loan with your financial institution and pay off your credit cards? That could reduce your interest rate by 15% per year or more. This saves you $1,500 per year on a $10,000 outstanding balance, not including the monthly compounding.

If you have a number of loans with similar interest rates, one strategy is to concentrate on those with a relatively short payback period, or the flexibility for extra payments. If you can vigorously attack one loan and get rid of it in a short period of time, you can then redirect those payments to the next loan, and so on. Bite off reasonable chunks that you can digest fairly quickly, rather than trying to eat the whole thing at once.

Oh yeah, you have to cut your spending and pinch pennies for a while. Did I mention that? (Actually, most people in that situation are eager to cut spending, if it means getting out of the mess more quickly.)

Once again, information is the key. Sit down and figure out where you spend all your money. List all your fixed expenses, list the ones where you have any flexibility at all, and start making some decisions.

Developing a spending plan and deciding where to spend your money is the first step toward putting you in charge.

Fixed costs, like utilities, don't have to stay fixed. You have some choices about how much cable TV you order, how much heat you use, and even the size and cost of your residence. People with serious debt problems have had to downsize their house for a period of time, but many have found it was the best thing they ever did.

They not only got out of debt, but also realized that they were perfectly happy—and sometimes much happier—in a living situation that cost 30% less. They use some of the extra cash flow now for travel, indulgences and future savings.

That's an option that can be looked at even if you aren't deep in debt, but it comes back to knowledge. Knowing your expenses will also help with predictability, as you budget for once-a-year expenses and try to put money aside every month or every paycheque for those one-time hits that used to put you in the red.

If you are behind on any bills, communicate pro-actively with your creditors. Let them know you understand the situation and you plan to take care of it. If you can't meet the minimum payment schedule, try to negotiate a new one. Don't expect them to be generous, but you will do better by contacting them before they assign you to a credit collection agency. That's when things get even uglier.

Here's a list of ways to make your dollars go further, courtesy of an article from Reader's Digest, in a sidebar called *How to Save $600 a Month*:

- avoid 'dry clean only' clothes—$50
- cut out cable—$40
- skip Friday night take-out—$80
- nix those Starbucks coffee breaks—$90
- clip grocery coupons, buy sale items in bulk, eschew prepared foods, and try generic brands—$120 for a family of four
- brown bag your lunch—$140 (also much healthier!)
- drop one club membership and jog, bike or swim—$50
- borrow videos and books from the library—$30

Some of these you might consider a temporary hardship, but others could easily be adopted long term, with no sacrifice. Think of what you could do with that money!

If you want to get serious about debt reduction, consider investing $22 in the book *Debt-Free Forever* by Gail Vaz-Oxlade. It provides a great step-by-step guide to tackling both large and small debt issues.

To get a little deeper into how your personality traits affect your financial decisions, the book *$pent* by Stephanie Holmes-Winton is very useful. You can order from www.ThemoneyFinder.ca.

Please don't be like an American politician and bury your head in the sand, or be paralyzed by what seems like an insurmountable task.

You can start slowly, and eat the bull elephant one bite at a time, but definitely start!

24

Gittin' a Lasso on Your Own Homestead

FOR ANY CANADIANS who have not yet purchased a home, the dream of home ownership is getting more difficult all the time. Twenty years of uninterrupted increases in house and condominium values has priced many people out of the market, some of them permanently.

Changes to the mortgage rules from 2010 to 2012 have also made it more difficult for first-time homeowners to finance their purchase, even if they can afford it.

However, I think that *realistic and affordable* home ownership is a very important component of achieving financial independence. It can be a very effective way of building equity, both from appreciation and by paying off the mortgage.

For other people, though, who buy more than they can afford and get caught by surprises like foundation repairs, leaking roofs or other major expenses when they are already pushed to the limit by mortgage payments and property taxes, it can be a disaster.

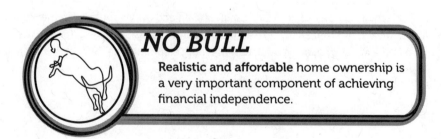

NO BULL

Realistic and affordable home ownership is a very important component of achieving financial independence.

Like everything else, purchase only what you can afford. If it turns out you "underbought," you will be able to build equity much faster, and with much less stress.

Over the past 10 years or so, with interest rates falling and then stabilizing at the lowest rates in history, another phenomenon has emerged among home-owners. This is the home equity line of credit (HELOC), otherwise known as "using your house as an ATM," and sucking out the equity every time it grows. This is done by increasing the line of credit backed by the home equity, and then borrowing more money.

Although this can be very useful when there is a good investment to make with the money or high interest rate debt that can be consolidated, you can tell I'm not a big fan of overdoing such borrowing. That's because most people use it to finance a lifestyle they cannot afford on their regular incomes.

Low interest rates have facilitated this, in the same way they have supported the unprecedented rise in house prices. Low rates allow people who could never get into a house if mortgage rates were 12.5% (the rate I paid on my first mortgage), to purchase a house, even at a purchase price twice what it was 10 years earlier.

A home can still be purchased with as little as 5% down payment. However, any down payment of less than 25% of the purchase price will require Canada Mortgage and Housing Corporation (CMHC) or similar insurance on the loan. This does not protect you, but rather protects the lending institution from default. Technically, the lending institution pays the insurance premium, but it is always added to the cost of the mortgage, which means the borrower actually pays.

In theory, the institution would lend to you without insurance, but charge a much higher interest rate. In practice, most institutions require insurance on such "high ratio" mortgages.

As you borrow a higher percentage of the purchase price, you pay a higher percentage of the mortgage value as a premium. For example, the premium is 0.65% of the total loan amount (1% if the borrower is self-employed) on a mortgage up to 75% of the value of the home.

If the loan to value ratio is above 90% up to 95%, the premium is 2.75% of the loan amount, and is not available at all to borrowers who are self-employed, without third party income validation.

Those premiums can add a lot to the costs of buying, though you can add the premiums to the mortgage instead of paying up front.

By the way, CMHC considers an acceptable down payment to be money from the purchaser's savings, RRSP withdrawal (hopefully under the RRSP Home-buyer's Plan), unencumbered land being built upon, and funds borrowed against other assets. "Sweat equity"—your own physical labour and expertise in building or organizing the building of the home—can also qualify, as can lender cash back incentives, or gifts from family or other's not tied to the seller. Maximizing the apparent down payment can be important, as keeping the mortgage to value ratio lower reduces the percentage charged and can significantly decrease the insurance premium.

Many tenants who are currently paying high amounts for rent could afford to pay mortgage payments, utilities and property taxes, if they were able to put together the down payment required to buy a house or condominium. That's the big challenge for most first-time home buyers.

Think back to Rita and Dan. If they want to buy a $300,000 house without having to pay CMHC mortgage insurance, they'll need 25% down, or $75,000. With a monthly cash flow surplus of say, $1,500, it would take them four years to save the down payment, by which time the house price might have risen 20%!

That's a classic treadmill.

So what's the solution for someone whose number one goal is home ownership?

CMHC helped us out by giving a list of potential sources of down payment funds. Many buyers these days are only in their house thanks to the largess of parents or other relatives. Occasionally, employers will loan money to key employees to help with the purchase of a house, especially if the employer has requested relocation.

For most buyers, a high ratio mortgage will be mandatory. In the most extreme example, Rita and Dan could borrow 95% of the house value, leaving a down payment requirement of only $15,000. (My advice to them would be to have at least another $5,000 available for closing costs and unexpected expenses, at a bare minimum, but let's leave that out for right now.)

The insurance premium would be 2.75% of the $285,000 mortgage, adding another $7,840 to the loan, for a total starting balance of $292,840. That's a razor thin amount of equity on a $300,000 house, even if they did not overpay at all. Equity will build slowly, but at least they're on the way.

So what will this shiny new mortgage cost?

If they're lucky enough to hit the jackpot with the lowest interest rates in history, in place at the time of this writing, they may be able to get a five-year closed mortgage, but with a variable interest rate, at 3.2%. If so, their monthly principal and interest payments will be $1,420, based on a 25-year amortization. (A five-year open variable rate mortgage carried an interest rate of 4% at the same time.)

Choosing a five-year fixed rate closed mortgage at 5.24% increases the monthly payments to $1,744.

Keep in mind that property taxes, heating, water, electrical and other utilities, phone, cable and maintenance are all on top of this, and must be factored into whether or not the total cost of housing is affordable.

In the case of Dan and Rita, they had $1,500 per month available as a surplus after paying rent and utilities on their rental house, which we will assume also totaled $1,500 per month. The new cost of ownership will be in the range of $2,000 per month, assuming they choose a variable rate or a one-year mortgage term and their total utilities and regular maintenance is kept under $500 per month.

That gives them a reasonable surplus to allow for contingencies and surprises, and might even give them the potential to do home improvements. That assumes all goes well. The reality of home ownership is that there are a lot of surprises and unanticipated expenses, which generally rise in direct proportion to the age of the house.

25

Can You Hold on if Interest Rates Rise?

IF YOU HAVE VARIABLE RATE DEBT, like lines of credit or a mortgage with a variable interest rate, immediately take stock of how your payments will change if interest rates go up, say, by 2% and by 4%.

For example, if you are currently paying 4% on a loan, become clear on the impact that a 6% and an 8% interest rate will have on that same loan. Depending on your loan structure, your payments might increase, or your amortization period might extend. Either way, get prepared now.

Just to give you perspective, from March 1994 to March 1995, the prime rate rose from roughly 5% to 9%. Variable rate loans rose by at least that much. Ouch.

If such an increase would stretch your budget, you've got a problem that you need to address. Locking in for a longer term right now is the obvious solution, but locking in means moving to a higher interest rate immediately. So how do you decide?

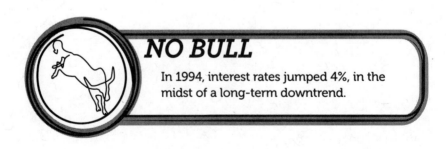

NO BULL

In 1994, interest rates jumped 4%, in the midst of a long-term downtrend.

The key is how badly you could be hurt by the rising rates. If a 2% or 3% rise in your rate will be a serious problem for you, look now at either locking in, consolidating your debts, or developing a specific strategy for reducing your debts over the next six to twelve months. (That's the ideal, and it might involve the novel idea of reducing spending.)

Some people will even look at breaking their current fixed rate mortgage with less than a year to run, in order to lock in at today's great rates.

Variable rate mortgages and loans are typically set at prime plus some percentage. As prime rises, so will the variable rate.

You will have to decide if you favour stability and guarantees over lower rates. If you are willing to share the risk with the lending institution, they will give you a lower rate.

Going back to our happy homeowners Rita and Dan, they seemed to have a reasonably comfortable margin of safety on top of their variable rate mortgage. However, if they chose the five-year rate guarantee, they paid an extra 2% and $324 per month right away. That makes a pretty compelling case to go with a variable rate mortgage, and allows general interest rates to rise 2% before catching up to the more conservative fixed-rate.

Our recommendation is, of course, to put aside that $324 to make extra payments on the mortgage and to build up an emergency fund, which can also act as an extra payment reserve if rates rise. If rates don't rise, and no other emergencies crop up, then some of that savings account can be used as an additional lump sum for the mortgage.

Be especially cautious about *investment* loans with variable rates—where you have leveraged your investments to purchase more with borrowed money—because often rising rates will hurt your investments at the same time as making your loan more expensive.

On your investments, be cautious about your exposure to bond funds or direct ownership of long-term bonds. The price of existing bonds goes down as interest rates rise, and the effect is more pronounced for longer-term bonds.

Or, put more correctly, bond prices go down when the bond market decides that the prospects for economic expansion are good and the market starts to anticipate that interest rates will rise in the future. These price adjustments happen on a daily basis in the bond market, but will result in a sustained depreciation of bond prices if rates start to rise consistently over a period of time.

In 1994, the average bond fund lost about 8% of its value. Your balanced funds also have a bond component.

Owning bonds or GICs directly, where you have a personal maturity value guarantee, allows you to ignore the short term drops and hold to maturity.

Equities and equity funds will generally rise in value significantly before interest rates rise significantly. Equities rise early in the expansion phase, before central governments become concerned about inflation or slowing the economy.

The biggest concern, however, is being up to your limit in variable interest rate debt. If you have any such exposure, do the calculation now to see what shape you'll be in if the interest rates on loans rise significantly.

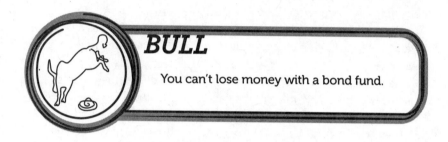

BULL

You can't lose money with a bond fund.

26

Good Debt vs Bad Debt: Make it Deductible!

"GOOD DEBT" is money borrowed to invest in something that is expected to increase in value, or would generate income in excess of the borrowing costs. This is positive leverage that can increase the rate at which you build wealth.

"Bad debt" is any money borrowed to purchase a depreciating asset, anything that gets used up or, perhaps worst of all, lifestyle adventures like vacations. Not only is the interest rate often higher, but the interest is never deductible and in the end, you are left only with the debt and little or nothing to show for it.

What about interest-free loans for cars or other consumer goods?

If you are being loaned money interest-free (or at 1% or 2%) to purchase an asset that you need, that would likely slide into the category of good debt, provided you can actually afford it. However, know that you are paying more than you would if you were paying cash. Someone is paying for the use of that money.

When you borrow to put money into an investment that will pay you income or provide the opportunity for future capital gains, generally the interest on the loan is deductible against your taxable income. This is another characteristic of good debt.

As a general philosophy, borrow to invest and pay cash for everything else.

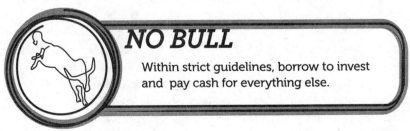

NO BULL

Within strict guidelines, borrow to invest and pay cash for everything else.

Using leverage also increases the risk you take when you invest, so you must be cautious. Always calculate—and be sure you can afford—the effect if the investment goes down and stays there for a period of time.

Using borrowed money to purchase a house can be worthwhile. However, the debt is not deductible, and therefore should be paid out as quickly as possible, even if it means replacing it with a deductible debt in the meantime.

This type of loan swap can be used to convert non-deductible to deductible over a series of years. Let's say you have a $100,000 mortgage and $20,000 in non-registered investments, or that you inherit $20,000.

Step one is to take the $20,000 and make an extra payment on the mortgage, assuming that large a payment can be made without penalty. You then set up a line of credit to purchase investments, either using the equity in your home or the investments themselves as collateral. The interest on this loan will be deductible, creating a small tax refund. You can either continue to use your surplus cash flow to pay down your mortgage and add to the investment loan for additional investment capacity, or you can withdraw growth from the investment plan to make extra payments on the mortgage.

Some strategies would have you borrow $100,000 to invest, have the income generated by the investment portfolio service the loan, while you take your annual tax refund and apply that to your mortgage. However, depending on the investment plan, to service the loan alone radically increases the dangers of leveraged investing.

The dangers and rewards of leveraged investing

So, should you borrow to invest?

My answer would be that if you are willing to borrow at all, borrowing to invest would clearly be the best reason to borrow. Any investment borrowing has to be within reason, which means that the payments are affordable and will continue to be affordable if interest rates take a significant rise. As well, your financial situation and the loan arrangement should both allow for considerable fluctuations in the investment value, **without** your loan being "called" and without your net worth being seriously damaged.

Loans taken out with investment dealers based on the value of investments in an account are called "margin" loans, and they will be called for repayment— or some of the investments sold at the wrong time—if the investment value falls below the margin allowance. The same thing can happen if the investment itself is the collateral for a bank loan.

The other big risk with borrowing to invest in a fluctuating investment is that you change your mind and sell the investment when its value is low. This is the classic case of buying high and selling low, sometimes also known as "chickening out."

To avoid this, you must have both the financial and psychological staying power needed to endure a prolonged bear market.

If you have $10,000 to invest and you borrow $10,000, thus giving you $20,000 to invest in mutual funds or blue chip stocks, you can use the investments as your only collateral. There are a number of loan programs available through investment dealers and financial institutions that will loan you a dollar for every two dollars of securities.

But if the investments decline in value, then you will have to add more money to maintain the loan ratio. If you don't have additional money to reduce the loan or add to the collateral, then your investments will be sold at a loss. Don't get in that position.

The way to avoid it is by initially borrowing well under the limit, or by providing alternate collateral like a mortgage on your home. Since the value of your home doesn't fluctuate as much, there is virtually no chance of a margin call.

One thing I am definitely against is the type of irresponsible leveraging that takes place in every bull market. This was repeated in the mid 1980s, late 1990s and 2006/2007 stock market booms, all just before a significant market crash. Each time, enthusiastic (and sometimes reckless) financial advisors have found it easy to convince people of the benefits of borrowing to invest. In the worst examples, people were borrowing against their homes to purchase mutual funds, and then using the funds they purchased with that loan as collateral for a 2-for-1 loan program. To compound the risk, withdrawals were being made from the mutual funds to service the debt.

Those houses of cards were bound to crumble, and many of them did. As soon as interest rates started rising, the debt service increased (which is a big risk to consider), and the rising rates pushed the stock market down at the same time.

Remember that leveraging magnifies any gains or losses on your investment, thus increasing the risk. If you can control that risk in the short term, then leveraging is a tool that can work for you.

If you have $5,000 to invest and then borrow $15,000, you have $20,000 exposed to the ups and downs of the market. When your total investment has grown by 25% to $25,000, you have actually doubled your money. Your $5,000 of original capital is now $10,000. Positive leverage. (Same thing happens when you borrow money to buy a house, and it grows in value.)

On the other hand, if the investment declines 20%, which is to be expected at some point in equity funds, you have lost 80% of your original investment.

Two rules to follow before using leverage:

1.   Only borrow to invest if you have excess cash flow and sincerely believe you will have the staying power, even in a two-year or three-year bear market.

2. Start a leverage program after a prolonged bear market, when no one else is investing and everyone thinks it's a bad idea. Do not borrow to invest after a long bull market.

If an investment salesman can show you that you would have made huge amounts of money in the last three years by investing in the market, that's not the time to start.

Either way, keep your debts good, and make sure they are deductible!

27

Is Leasing the "Crack Cocaine" of Car Nuts?

I THINK I'LL BUY a convertible. The ads in today's paper say that I can buy for no money down and just make teeny, tiny payments every month, and immediately look great, and be more attractive to the opposite sex.

Can it really be that easy?

When you see itty bitty payments advertised, you can usually be certain that a lease is being offered, instead of a purchase. So why are the payments so much lower?

When you lease a car, you pay only for the *use* of the car for a period of time, not the car itself. When you *buy* a car, you buy the whole thing and own it in the end, and therefore must pay more over the same time period.

For example, leasing a $25,000 car on a two-year lease means that you have purchased the use of the car for two years, and then you give it back. There are two components to that cost—the depreciation factor and the finance charges. If the car is worth $15,000 when you give it back, you have only "used up" $10,000 of car use and financed a $10,000 loan.

You have also built up zero equity. You own nothing.

As you know, car values depreciate very steeply as soon as you drive them off the lot, and they continue to depreciate rapidly for the next few years. (After three years or so, the rate of depreciation each year levels out substantially, so the smart money buys used.)

At the end of the lease, you do not actually own anything except the first right to purchase the car at the *residual value*. This is the estimated value after depreciation at the end of the term of the lease.

When leasing, make sure you understand the actual finance rate and all charges, as this used to be the way leasing companies made a lot of profit, by charging very high interest rates. That's not as common anymore, but one thing I know from my car dealer friends is that they make more money from leasing than they do from selling.

As well, be clear on the number of kilometres you are allowed to drive during the term of the lease. If you exceed the allowable amount, the charges are quite high. Finally, understand your "gap coverage," which is insurance that pays the difference between what you owe on the lease and what your vehicle is actually worth, if your vehicle is destroyed or stolen. You don't want to be left paying the difference.

This raises an interesting point, though, doesn't it? The fact that the car will be worth less than you owe on it after two or three years should be very scary, and brings with it a lesson.

My son just told me about his friend who bought a brand-new Kia—surely a sensible car—on a five-year loan arrangement. When the car was totaled in an accident two years later, the insurance company paid the owner $3,000 less than the car was worth. The poor kid was not only left carless, but still owed the bank $3,000!

Being approved for automobile financing **does not** mean you can afford the car, and it certainly does not mean that such a purchase is a good idea.

A big attraction to leasing—or even buying with no money down and a five-year or six-year payment plan—is that you can get a lot more car than if you wait to save and pay cash. As a financial planner, I see that as the huge danger. Cars are not an investment; they are a cost—a depreciating asset. They get used up.

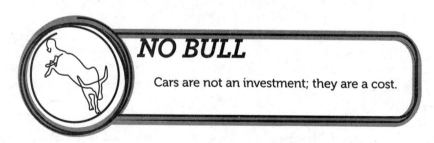

NO BULL

Cars are not an investment; they are a cost.

An actual advantage to leasing compared to buying is that you don't pay the GST, PST or HST up front, and instead pay those taxes only monthly as you make your lease payments. You still pay them, but they are spread out over time.

So, should you lease or should you buy? In some circles, the traditional wisdom is that you "buy what goes up; rent (or lease) what goes down." Based on this, one would lease a depreciating asset like a car, and buy an appreciating asset, like real estate.

I agree with that approach, except for one major factor—it's tough to lease a used car.

My philosophy is that you let someone else take the big depreciation, by buying a car that's two or three years old, but with warranty remaining. In the next couple of years, you should have a pretty good idea of the reliability factor, and can continue to own it or move on to another one.

My family cars have both just turned eight and 12 respectively. We bought each of them when they were four years old. We are obviously off warranty, but repairs have been minimal, perhaps because we bought very high-quality cars. We could afford that, because we let someone else pay for the new car depreciation. Both cars are still worth 60% to 70% of what we paid, after owning them for more than six years. People who bought new cars at the same time have generally lost three quarters of their value.

The details? I drive a 2005 Lexus IS 300 SportCross. When Lexus introduced this car in 2002, I test drove one and fell in love with it. But I could never bring myself to spend that much on a car. So I waited some six years until it became affordable for me, and I could pay cash for it, along with my trade in. (By the way, I could have done better selling the old car myself than trading it in, which is what I recommend if you have the time.)

This is actually my second nice car, not including my vintage BMW 2002 that I bought for $1,600 when I was 20. My breakthrough came at age 48, when my daughter totaled my six-year-old Honda. (The good news was that we had trained our kids well, so Sarah's first sentence on the phone was, "Dad, I'm fine...no one is hurt..." before the bad news about the car.) With that "opportunity," I finally indulged my lifelong passion for cars, and found a five-year-old Volvo S80 T6 twin turbo powerhouse, with a retail value of $63,000.

My purchase price? I paid just $23,000, and they threw in a set of winter tires.

That doesn't speak to the buy-or-lease subject, but hopefully will motivate you to be patient. For me it's been worth it, as I smile every time I walk toward my car, and literally giggle every time I drive it.

To make a proper comparison between buying and leasing, get all the facts and compare the options side by side. There is no absolute answer, and you may find that it comes down to the price and age of the car.

Leasing is a good idea for those who have a good business reason to drive a new car and to turn them over frequently. Leasing mitigates residual value risk.

Car dealers will tell you that people who need their car to earn income—like real estate or other salespeople—and can therefore deduct some costs from their taxes—should lease. However, a purchaser can also deduct a portion of the interest component on monthly payments and deduct capital cost allowance, so the net tax benefits are actually similar.

When leasing, a portion of the lease cost is deductible, based on the percentage of business use versus personal use. (In both cases, of course, CRA insists you keep proper records, which include the date, destination, purpose and number of kilometers relevant to each trip. Travelling from your home to work and back does **not** qualify as business use.)

With both buying and leasing, there's a limit to the maximum deductible value, currently based on a manufacturer's suggested retail price (MSRP) of $35,294, plus HST (or GST and PST), or a maximum monthly lease cost of $800 plus HST (or GST and PST). The CRA website (http://www.cra-arc.gc.ca/tx/ndvdls/tpcs/ncm-tx/rtrn/cmpltng/ddctns/lns206-236/229/cmmssn/vhcl-eng.html) has all the rules and charts to work out the limits.

What does it really cost?

So you think you're ready for your luxury dream car? Well then, let's take a look at the actual costs, using an Infinity G35X as our sample. This is a practical Canadian car, with all-wheel drive and a very sophisticated traffic control system to get the power to the ground in the winter.

A couple of years ago, the MSRP on the premium model was $47,954 (exactly twice the cost of my first house). If I purchase the car outright, there will be $2,397 of GST and $3,357 of Manitoba PST at 7%, for a grand total of $53,709. If I put $2,000 down on a purchase and finance the balance over four years, my monthly payments will be $1,160 and I'll own the car outright in four years. Payments total $55.760, for interest costs of $1,971.

If I take out a two-year lease, my monthly payments will be $1,041, including GST and PST. After two years, I can either give the car back or purchase it for $28,293, plus taxes. Paying cash to buy the car at that point would make the total cost with the taxes $56,672, plus interest on any loan required at that point. So, leasing and then buying out after the two year lease would increase the total purchase price by less than $1,000. This assumes you do not drive more than the kilometers allowed in the agreement, in which case you would face stiff penalties. Make sure the mileage allowance fits your needs, or purchase "gap insurance."

If I wanted to minimize my cash outflow I could opt for a four-year lease, lowering my payments to $762. My buyout value at the end would be $20,620, or I could simply give the car back and start a lease on a brand new one. This increases the cost somewhat more, but means less cash outflow in the early year.

It is this lower initial monthly payment that can be addictive to a car nut.

Naturally, I was careful to ask the interest rate. The four year terms were both 3.9%, while the two year lease was 2.9%.

The financial planner in me has to point out that the best thing to do is to wait two years until the market value is $28,293, in the meantime investing the $1,041 monthly lease cost into a money market fund. That would give you $25,000 plus a bit of interest in two years. You could then pay cash for the car, when you can actually afford it.

Neither the most persuasive salesperson nor the most seductive new car smell can convince me this isn't a better choice.

Whether you lease or buy, don't overspend.

NO BULL

Whether you lease or buy, only commit to the car you can afford.

Managing the Bull:
Detect and Deflect the Crap

YOUR VISION FOR YOUR LIFE should govern your overall strategies and your spending choices. If you decide—right now—that you are going to be financially secure and always in control of your finances, and you commit to that vision, then that vision will help you with all of your financial choices.

Being in control of your own destiny and getting ahead financially will often mean delaying gratification. This means waiting to buy something until you can afford to pay for it. In our experience with hundreds of clients, delaying gratification in this way inevitably means deeper and longer lasting satisfaction with whatever the money is ultimately used to purchase.

That sounds like a win-win situation, and it is.

Establishing the habit of sensible financial management early will almost guarantee a life of plenty, with less stress, lower interest costs and far fewer financial mistakes. This habit is usually established with small decisions and purchases, and ultimately carries over to the big decisions.

Smart use of credit, whether with credit cards, lines of credit or house mortgages, can save you thousands of dollars of interest and other finance charges and lead to financial independence years earlier.

A little common sense and No Bull thinking is really all it takes.

Part 4

Growing Your Herd:
Insider Tips on Investing

*"Don't gamble. Take all your savings and buy
a good stock, and hold it till it goes up, then sell it.
If it don't go up, don't buy it."*

– WILL ROGERS, AMERICAN HUMOURIST

28

What Makes a Successful Bull Rider or Investor?

YOU HAVE HEARD of the "legendary investor", and champion bull rider Warren Buffett. While some of his incredible success can be chalked up to good timing and good luck, there are also several traits that helped him to be incredibly successful. You can adopt these, as well.

Other lesser known (but arguably more impressive) investing heroes like Peter Lynch, David Dreman and many others, have exhibited similar characteristics and behaviours. It may be helpful to look at some of the traits they had in common, that helped them achieve their success. Many of their techniques will also work for you!

Courage and patience are both needed. All have demonstrated patience by waiting to buy their target investments until the prices became reasonable, even at times when the mass of the investing public was clamoring for certain stocks—or for the stock market in general—driving up the prices to levels which no longer represented good value.

I remember clearly hearing David Dreman speak in late 1999, when tech stocks like Cisco, JDS Uniphase and Nortel were trading at incredible multiples of profit, and 'idea' stocks like pets.com were selling out IPOs at stratospheric prices with no profits or even an operating business. At the time, JDS, Nortel and one other tech darling had a collective market capitalization that valued them more highly than *all* of the Canadian banks, mining and oil companies and retailers **combined**. That skewed valuation was what "the market" was saying these "new economy" stocks were worth at that time. By bidding these prices up so high, the market said these few companies making widgets that supported the infrastructure of the internet, were worth more than all of the rest of corporate Canada.

There were new investment management heroes being minted monthly, as these "geniuses" who invested their clients' money in these over-priced but rising stocks were temporarily generating annual returns of 70% or more.

Managers like Dreman and Buffett were being criticized for missing out on this new paradigm, where the belief was that tech and dot com company profits would be so huge that conventional measures of valuation were out the window.

Both of these managers (and some others) refused to play this game. Dreman said he thought these valuations made no sense (I think the word he used was "crazy"), and instead invested very cheaply in profitable companies that the market was ignoring. As the prices of those conventional stocks fell even more, he looked like a has-been, but he stuck to his common sense approach. This was the clearest example of the behaviours that earned him the label "contrarian" over the years. His decisions were often contrary to the crowd.

At the same time, Buffett was politely saying that he didn't really understand these companies, their high tech businesses or the valuations the market was putting on them, and he made it his policy to not invest in businesses he did not understand.

He had made piles of money for himself and his investors in the 1990s with companies like National Indemnity Company, Coca-Cola and Dairy Queen. But when his company Berkshire Hathaway started falling behind the tech craze, the business media also started to label Buffett as yesterday's man.

Exercising the kind of restraint that such managers showed at that time, when their clients and investors were clamoring to get on an easy money bandwagon, took courage as well as patience.

But the real courage is needed when choosing to invest money and buy stocks when the market is in a selling panic, like late 2008 and early 2009. Buying stocks when no one wants them, or "when there is blood in the streets," as Buffett likes to describe it, is a real test of nerve and commitment to one's ideas.

Your investment choices will not be attacked in such a public way, but courage and patience will still be critical to you in your success as an investor. This does NOT mean taking crazy chances or making high-risk investments. Instead, it means maintaining ownership of high quality, commonsense investments, even when the market drives their price down.

It means having the courage to buy those high-quality investments when the market is afraid of them, when you can buy them for attractive prices. It may mean having the courage to sell investments when it is obvious that the market is starting to ignore risk and disregard value, and has bid prices up to ridiculous levels.

Investing success will also come from having patience. In your case, this will likely mean putting away a small amount of money every month for years, and maintaining that investing discipline through bad markets as well as good. In fact, bad markets are where you can really lay the foundation to make serious money later on, using the investment methods outlined in the coming pages.

It's not just about patience and courage. There are many more reasons why some people are successful investors, while others are not.

A few do well on their own; others do well with professional advice. There are other investors, however, who do poorly—or disastrously—either on their own or with an advisor. Why?

When we look at the factors that lead to investing success, we find contradictions, but many consistent principles, as well. Much has to do with psychology. Successful investors are good at controlling their impulses, and do not act just on emotion. It's very easy to get excited about a great idea, and jump on it without proper research and sober second thought. Good investors take that time to reflect.

At the same time, listening to your "gut feeling" can be very valuable. If an investment idea just doesn't "feel right" to you, best to take a pass on it, even if you are not completely clear on why you feel that way. This is quite different than being emotional and following impulses.

To be successful in any endeavour, it also helps to take personal responsibility for outcomes, as opposed to blaming other people or circumstances when things go wrong. Even the best investors make mistakes, but the good ones get value from those mistakes by "owning" them and learning from them.

Some investors expect their advisors to be able to predict accurately the future, which they cannot. Those investors are angry with their advisors when the market goes down and their investments decline in value. The investors might put in place an investment plan that has always worked over five year cycles, and then get impatient or panic when it is not working after two years.

Such investors often change their advisor, their investments or their investing strategy, at just the wrong time.

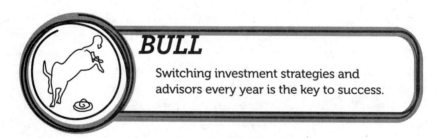

BULL

Switching investment strategies and advisors every year is the key to success.

Lesson—try to be clear about what is going on in the investment environment, and separate facts from myth, before reacting. And then *respond*, don't just *react*.

NO BULL

Successful investors control their impulses, and listen to their instincts.

Your *instincts* can be powerful, but your *impulses* may be damaging or dangerous, if acted upon thoughtlessly.

Some investors abandon a successful long-term investment strategy, because they find it "boring" or because they have heard from a friend about a recent "home run." Those investors should carefully examine their motivation, and perhaps work out their gambling urges in a safer forum. In those circumstances, it would be wise to set aside a small and limited amount of your portfolio for your "play money," which you can use to satisfy those impulses.

Lesson—be clear on *why* you are investing. If it is to make money over time and achieve your retirement goals, then great. You will likely make many good decisions.

On the other hand, if you are really motivated by the excitement of the "game," and it's all about hitting home runs and having a great stock market killing to brag about at cocktail parties, then you may need to turn your core investments over to a professional manager.

From my observation of hundreds of successful professional and amateur investors over 30 years, the real keys are:

1. Follow the investment planning process,
2. Keep your emotions (either positive or negative) from sending you down a different path from the one you have set, and
3. Do your best to stay out of the way while your investment plan and the vehicles you've chosen do their jobs.

There are all sorts of tactical adjustments, investment techniques and secrets we will share in the coming chapters, but throughout, it's important that you keep these fundamentals in mind. This approach might not make you a star at cocktail parties in the short run, but 10 years from now you'll be the one gloating.

29

The Investment Planning Process— How to Stay on the Bull

AS YOU HAVE LIKELY NOTICED, we folks in financial planning tend to be process-oriented. So, not surprisingly, we have a clearly defined process for planning out your investment portfolio.

Many investors (and even advisors) approach investing from completely the wrong direction, looking first at new or "hot" products or listening to stock tips and then buying an investment vehicle, only then trying to figure out how it fits into the portfolio, and finally looking at whether or not the entire portfolio is appropriate for that investor's situation and goals.

Instead, we recommend first defining those personal goals, your rate of return needs and comfort level, using that knowledge to determine the right mix of asset classes, putting the resulting investment policy in writing, then determining the best overall tax and fee structure and only **then** looking at the individual investment products that can fill that prescription.

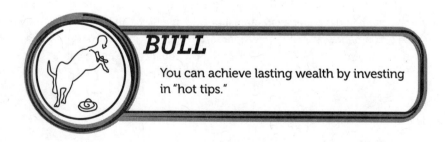

BULL

You can achieve lasting wealth by investing in "hot tips."

Here's more detail on the process and the steps we recommend:

1. **Determine your investor risk profile.** This is highly personal, and based on individual factors like your time horizon, your need for current income (if any) from the portfolio, your need for liquidity, and your risk tolerance, which is based on both financial and psychological factors.

    Virtually all advisors have questionnaires they use to help bring out the unique aspects of your situation and use the collection of them to determine a score for you.

2. **Decide on your ideal asset mix.** Both your risk profile and your personal ideal asset mix are based on the details of your own situation, not external factors like someone's projections of interest rates, economic growth rates or stock market direction. (Those forecasts are wrong more than half the time, anyway.) We strongly recommend that you document these asset mix decisions in a written Investment Policy Statement (IPS) that will guide you and your advisors in maintaining a consistent approach, which is so important to your long term investing success.

    A crude example of a target asset mix is:

Cash and near cash	12%
Fixed income	32%
Equity	56%
	100%

    The IPS should also describe the frequency of re-balancing, and what degree of variation from target will result in a portfolio adjustment.

3. **Design the most tax-effective portfolio structure possible.** Generally, place tax-advantaged investments like stocks in your taxable accounts and only earn interest in tax-sheltered areas, like RRSP's.

    The dividends paid on stocks and preferred shares attract the dividend tax credit when held outside registered accounts, significantly decreasing the effective tax rate on the investment income. As well, part of the expected return on stocks comes from capital appreciation. This growth is tax free until the stock is sold, and when sold, only half the gain is included in taxable income.

    Interest on fixed income investments like GICs, bonds and treasury bills are fully taxed if held outside registered accounts, so are best owned inside the tax shelter.

4. **Decide on your preferred management options.** The choices range from doing it all yourself with the help of a newspaper and an Internet connection, using a discount broker, or investing with the help of a planner or investment advisor (IA), either through a mutual fund dealer or a full-service investment dealer. With a large portfolio—typically $250,000 or much larger—investors can hire a full-time professional portfolio manager. This is a person or a firm to

whom you give the authority to make investment decisions and trades, based on your agreed upon IPS.

5. **Choose investments.** Finally, we get to the selection of individual investment products and vehicles. If you make these selections at this point in the process, they will automatically fit into the structure you have designed. The choices are then more obvious, with decisions much easier to make and usually much more appropriate.

    The first level of selection is related to Step 4. You might want to pick individual stocks and bonds—either by yourself or with the help of a manager or IA—or you might prefer the convenience of mutual funds. Additional options have become available in the last five to 10 years. These include separately managed accounts or SMAs, where a manager picks the individual stocks and bonds which are then shown in the investor's accounts. There are also pooled funds, which are similar to mutual fund trusts, but offered by offering memorandum rather than prospectus, and generally intended for larger portfolios, and offer lower fees.

6. **Periodic reviews.** As with the rest of your financial plan, you must periodically review your asset mix, your investments and your approach, to make sure that these have kept pace with your changing situation.

    This does not mean looking at your portfolio daily or weekly, which is likely to drive you crazy and lead to bad decisions. A thorough review quarterly, with re-balancing your asset mix, is likely ideal. Annually, you should ask yourself if your overall asset mix and strategy is still appropriate for your situation. Do not change your IPS simply because the markets have gone up, or the markets go down.

    Change your target asset mix only when something about your situation has changed, or if you realize the original mix was inappropriate for you in some way.

30

The Eight Second Lesson on How the Stock Market Works

WHEN YOU BUY A COMPANY—in this case, let's pretend you could buy the whole thing—you expect to get a return on your money invested. You may be paid a salary if you work in the business, or maybe just receive a share of the profits. You also hope you will be able to make that company grow, improve its customer base, increase profits and eventually sell the company for a profit.

When you buy a whole company, you may also have to manage it, worry personally about employees and customers, and maybe even worry about employing family members or passing the business on to them in the future. To sell down the road, you must find a buyer and negotiate the sale, which includes items like the price and the terms of payment.

Buying part of a good business through stock investing

To solve some of these management and liquidity issues, and to provide capital for business to expand more quickly, the public capital markets—the stock exchanges—were created. These are "places" where willing buyers and sellers of company shares come together, **bid** for shares, **ask** for a certain price, and **trade**, through investment dealer intermediaries.

Your purpose as an investor, in participating in this market, is to be able to buy shares in companies that you think are well-managed, have strong balance sheets, are growing their earnings, and have a particular niche or strategic advantage in their business area or market.

You are able to make an investment appropriate to your situation, and you don't have to buy the whole company. You can, therefore, buy shares of several companies to diversify your investment eggs into several baskets.

As a shareholder in a public company, you have equity—ownership—but you don't have to worry about management or succession issues. Selling your shares is no problem, as most exchange-listed companies trade millions of shares every day, ensuring liquidity. That is the whole purpose of the stock market. You can sell when you want, if you are willing to accept the price that is bid at that time. Or, you can hold out for a better bid.

Your purpose in equity investing is to seek a return on your money, through dividends and/or capital gains. Let's see what that looks like.

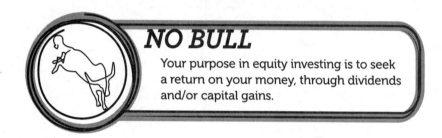

NO BULL

Your purpose in equity investing is to seek a return on your money, through dividends and/or capital gains.

Tax treatment

Many mature companies pay **dividends**. These are a cash payment (or sometimes payments in more stock) paid to shareholders, usually every three months. Large companies have already paid corporate tax at a high rate, and so they are able to pay "eligible" dividends to shareholders. Eligible dividends are taxable, but also create a large dividend tax credit to offset some, or even all, of the tax on the dividend.

For taxpayers with less than $40,000 or so of taxable income, the tax rate on dividends is *negative* in most provinces. This means that the dividend tax credit provides more cash to the taxpayer than the amount of tax on the dividend.

This is a tremendous advantage for the individual taxpayer investor, reflecting the fact that the company already paid tax on the same earnings at a high rate.

In Ontario, the effective tax rate on eligible dividends "jumps" to 13.4% for taxpayers whose total net taxable incomes are above $42,000, and goes to 14.2% on taxable income between $68,700 and $78,000. Still pretty attractive.

For higher income earners, the tax rate on eligible dividends (EDs) is 25.4%, on taxable income from $85,400 to $132,000, and 29.5% on income from $132,000 to $500,000. In 2012, Ontario introduced a new tax bracket above $500,000 of taxable income, at which level EDs are taxed at 31.69%, and Manitoba increased its top tax rate on EDs to 32.26%.

(The tax principal at work here is called "integration." The system is designed so that the combined taxes of a corporation and a shareholder receiving dividends are not higher than if the shareholder were to receive all of their income as salary, instead. It's not perfect, but it comes close.)

The corresponding figures for interest income are 31% for middle income earners to a maximum of 46.4% for taxable incomes from $132,000 to $500,000, and almost 48% for people in the new Ontario top tax bracket. Perhaps most importantly, interest income is taxed at 20% on taxable income between $10,800 and $39,000, while the rate for eligible dividends is **negative** 1.9%. (Before Manitoba's changes this year, the first two tax brackets resulted in a negative tax rate on EDs.)

In Alberta, the maximum tax rate on eligible dividends is 19.3%, versus 39% for interest. For taxable income up to $42,000, interest is taxed at 25%, while dividends are tax-free.

Each province's tax rates and tax bracket thresholds are different and tend to change every year with inflation indexing. These figures given are for illustration only, but show accurately the relative advantage of eligible dividend income, compared to interest income, in a taxable account.

Some shareholders who are trying to accumulate long-term wealth instead of collecting regular income now choose a Dividend Reinvestment Plan (DRIP) to re-invest their dividends automatically in more shares. The dividend is still taxable, but this no-cost additional investment is a great growth technique.

Capital gains are only reported when the gain is realized, at the time when the shares are sold or there is a "deemed disposition." So, you can buy a share for $10, and hold it for 20 years, during which time it might grow to be worth $40, and you will have paid no tax on that growth until you sell or dispose of the share.

Very likely, the dividend will have increased several fold during that period of time, which is the real long-term win for most people. In the example above, the stock might have been paying a forty cent per year dividend when purchased, but is now paying three dollars per share per year. So, a $10,000 investment in 2014 which is paying $400 per year in dividends might be paying $3,000 per year in 2034.

That's the long-term value of ownership and equity.

People who set up a DRIP plan and use the dividends along the way to purchase additional shares might have also doubled or tripled the number of shares they own, turning that retirement income into $6,000 or $9,000 per year in 2034. That's a heck of a lot better deal than owning a bond or GIC with a fixed interest rate of $400 per year, even if you were reinvesting the interest each year.

Good quality dividend paying stocks are a great way to beat inflation and build future retirement income.

Now, doesn't that sort of long-term planning make a lot more sense than trying to time the stock market, and trying to find opportunities for bragging at cocktail parties about your short-term gains and losses?

31

Making it to the Bell:
A Real-Life Story of Riding
the Championship Bull

THERE ARE DIFFERENT METHODS of investing in shares other than direct ownership, and we will explore those shortly. But I want to first outline a true life story that will illustrate the risks and rewards of equity investing.

I know a couple—we'll call them Bob and Carol—who did well saving and investing throughout their careers, and then retired at age 60, in 2006. Carol started to receive her teacher's pension as a monthly income, which provides about one-third of their regular needs. Bob chose instead to transfer his pension money out into a personal investment portfolio, which his pension plan allowed. When this was combined with their existing RRSP and non-registered investments, the portfolio was worth almost exactly $1 million. Bob started drawing regular income from each of those accounts.

So far, nothing too unusual, right?

Here's where it gets a little more interesting.

Bob decided to maintain his accumulation investment policy of 100% equity investments—**all stocks**—so did not make any changes due to his retirement. His logic was that the 28 Canadian blue chip stocks he owned were paying dividends of more than 4% on average, and he was confident they would keep paying those dividends. Over time, he also believed the companies would keep increasing their dividends, which all had done in the six years he had owned the stocks.

When combined with Carol's pension, the dividends provided all of the income the couple needed, so they were not depending on capital gains. As Bob put it, "The stocks are like apartment buildings with good tenants. I don't care if the real estate market goes up or down, as long as I can keep collecting and increasing my rents to beat inflation."

OK, makes sense... but then came 2008.

You remember 2008? Global financial crisis, falling stock markets, bankrupt financial institutions... it's all coming back to you now?

Bob's portfolio value dropped in half. Ouch. I spoke to him then and, although shaken, he decided to stick to his approach. The dividends kept coming, so why change? Only one of his companies had cut its dividend in half, while the other 27 had all maintained their dividends at the same rate.

It's a happy ending, of course. Bob's stock values are back above the 2006 levels, and almost every company he owns is now paying *a higher dividend* than in 2008. Bob and Carol's total income is therefore up, keeping pace with rising costs. As a bonus, they no longer experience any anxiety when the stock market falls, as it's no longer their first rodeo.

Now, I don't recommend this approach of 100% equity investing, and it's *not* the one we use with our clients. We make sure that our clients' portfolios are more balanced, and therefore are never hit with such drops in value. Having fixed income and short-term investments on the sidelines also allows tactical adjustments to take advantage of market cycles, by using the cash to buy more shares at a low price. Our approach certainly means less stress for clients.

Anyone who takes Bob and Carol's approach also needs to have cash reserves and other safety measures in place.

This extreme—but real life—example shows how equity investing can pay off, in spite of the worst stock markets in 60 years. However, Bob and Carol rode it till the bell. They didn't bail out halfway through the ride.

By investing 100% of their portfolio in stocks without diversifying into safer asset classes, they took the championship bull by the horns, with no rodeo clowns to help them off when things got rough.

Here's a certainty to keep in mind—only choose to fully mount the bull without a net, as Bob and Carol did, if you are certain you can hang in till the bell. Bailing out halfway through the ride will almost always result in losses.

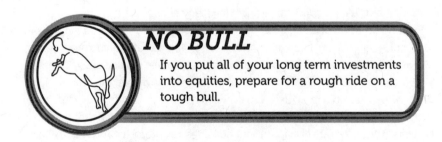

NO BULL

If you put all of your long term investments into equities, prepare for a rough ride on a tough bull.

32

Don't Put All Your Bulls in One Pasture— Introduction to Diversification

HERE'S THE THING—stocks and other ownership investments like real estate and businesses are what will build your wealth long-term. But stocks go down as well as up, and sometimes stay down for several years. That's a great time to be buying stocks, but the worst time to be selling them.

Proper diversification means owning different classes of investments that will do well at different times. Diversification also means making sure you have adequate reserves of guaranteed liquid investments to fund any of your potential needs for cash in the short term. This avoids being forced to sell stocks at the wrong time.

Always remember Dave's Rule Number One of Investing—**Never put yourself in a position where you have to sell low.**

Some years are exceptional. There is no escaping the fact that 2008 was a terrible year to be an investor. Even some guaranteed investments (like asset-backed commercial paper) cost some investors money, at least in the short run.

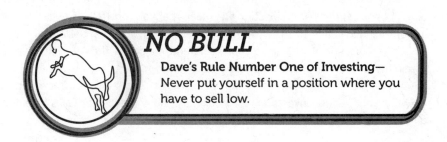

NO BULL

Dave's Rule Number One of Investing—
Never put yourself in a position where you have to sell low.

Formerly safe investments like good quality corporate bonds and preferred shares had unprecedented declines, so even conservative portfolios were savaged. There were very few places to hide.

So imagine my surprise when the majority of my clients reacted positively to their 2008 year-end performance reports! The best was a letter from a client that said, literally, "You guys rock!"

Hadn't had that comment before....

Clients were greatly relieved when we showed them their actual overall returns. A lot of it comes down to expectations and being realistic about the climate in which we were investing.

If you expected a return of negative 40% to 50%, because that's how much the major stock markets declined, you are pleasantly surprised when you are "only" down 17.7%, which was the average of our client returns in 2008.

More importantly, they all had enough guaranteed investments to carry them through two to five years of bear market.

It seems this diversification thing works, with the number one principle being to have enough cash reserves to ride out storms. Our approach is to have enough money in cash and guaranteed investments to cover at least two years of the client's expected withdrawals, and then have a segment of fixed income invest-ments (bonds or GICs) with guaranteed maturity values to cover off years three to five.

In all cases, it doesn't matter whether you own your investments directly or you own them through mutual funds. If you have a mutual fund that invests in government treasury bills, then you have a cash-like investment. If you have a mutual fund that invests in stocks, then you have an equity investment.

Diversification means balance, and hedging your bets. Diversifying between the three main asset classes we mentioned, diversifying geographically by investing in a number of countries rather than just Canada, spreading out your maturity dates on fixed income investments, investing in a number of companies rather than just a few and purchasing mutual funds that utilize a variety of invest-ment styles are all methods of diversifying your portfolio.

The goal of diversification is to smooth out the returns and manage the various different risks. Proper diversification will mean that your portfolio is never the top performing one in any given year, but it will never be the poorest performer either. Ideal diversification will achieve your goals and maximize the returns possible, within the level of risk that your situation allows.

When diversifying, make sure that you have established genuine differences between your various investments. For example, buying five-year GICs from four different institutions is not diversification, as all will perform the same way if interest rates are low in five years. More effective would be putting one fifth of the investments into each of one to five year GICs.

Similarly, purchasing three different mutual funds, each of which invests only in the Toronto Stock Exchange composite index, is not very good diversification. It's very likely these funds will behave in a similar fashion to each other, unless they have very different styles of investment selection. It would be more effective to put one-third of the money into a US stock fund, and one-third into an international fund, for example.

Our **cash reserves** approach allows us to comply with Dave's Rule Number One of Investing. It means always avoiding getting into a position where you may have to sell a fluctuating investment to generate cash, at a time when that investment is down, instead of up.

(The exception is selling to realize a capital loss for tax purposes, but then you will likely buy back a similar investment to participate in the expected recovery.)

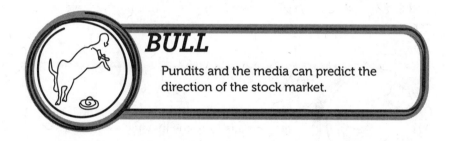

BULL

Pundits and the media can predict the direction of the stock market.

Do we set cash and fixed income aside even when "markets are good," and even though interest rates are low?

Yes, absolutely, because *NO ONE* ever knows what the markets are going to do tomorrow. We always have to prepare for the worst, because there is no accurate warning sign to say, "Markets will fall this year." I would argue that there is more risk in "good" times, when the market has been rising for years without a break, than there is at a time like now, when everyone knows about the economic problems facing the world, and stock prices are low as a result.

So did these principles apply in 2009, after an historic market decline, when everyone should have been piling into equities to make their money back? And did these principles apply in 2010, after an historic market recovery, and a growing sense that stock prices would keep rising?

Yes, the principle of always keeping enough in short term and guaranteed investments to satisfy your cash and income needs always applies, even if it means moving a small amount of your equities out of the market when it's necessary to re-balance your portfolio, or to maintain your cash reserves.

I repeat, no one knows where the markets will go tomorrow or the rest of the year. The goal of your investment planning is to limit the damage from the inevitable declines and maximize the participation in the recoveries. Strategic asset class investing assists you in that. Holding cash reserves gives you a place to draw on in emergencies, if those emergencies occur when it's a bad time to sell equities. Reserves also give you "dry powder" to use when a market crash presents you with historic buying opportunities.

The headlines about the economy do not accurately tell you where the markets are going or what is going to happen in the future, nor do the predictions of economists or analysts. Your only protection is proper diversification, common sense, and avoiding letting market euphoria suck you into committing too much money to equities when the market is high.

If your investment portfolio were your garden shed, you would need to have both a lawn mower and a snowblower, because in investing, we never know what the weather will be tomorrow.

NO BULL

The goal of your investment planning is to limit the damage from the inevitable declines and maximize the participation in the recoveries.

33

The Art of Strategic Asset Allocation— Choosing your Herd

WHEN WE TALK ABOUT asset classes in investing, we refer initially to the three main ones:

1. Cash and short term investments—guaranteed investments coming due within one year
2. Fixed income—bonds and GICS—which is *loaning* your money
3. Equities, or stocks—which is *owning* an asset or business

Between 70% and 90% of your rate of return in any particular given year is attributable to the asset class in which you are invested, rather than the particular investment you have made within that class. This means that in a year when stocks go up strongly, almost all stocks rise. In a year when bonds fall due to rising interest rates, it is likely that all bonds will fall.

There are always exceptions, like some stocks that far outperform or underperform their class in a given period of time, but the general rule still holds from year to year.

If the asset class determines our returns, then why don't we just invest in the proper class each year? Well, it's not that easy. That would be the Will Rogers school of investing.

Over half of the predictions of economists, market analysts and other gurus are wrong in any given year. If you look back over the last few decades you can see that there was really no predictability about which asset class was going to perform the best in any given year. Sometimes the top performer is cash, even when interest rates are under 2%. Who would have predicted that? Sometimes the top performer is fixed income and sometimes it's equities.

Here are some specific numbers about past returns. Remember that past returns do not guarantee future returns. However, they can teach us a lot about humility.

The best one-year return in the last 30 years was 79% in 1982/1983. There was a gain of 51% in the year ending September 2000. Both of these results came after bad markets, with the one-year return to June 30, 1982 being the worst in the last 30 years, at negative 42%.

That's why we don't go into the stock market with money we want to cash in for next winter's vacation, do we, ladies and gentlemen? The patterns also teach us that the extraordinary returns always come on the rebound from a correction or crash, when virtually all hope has been abandoned.

On average, the one-year return on the TSX has been 7.68%. However, the "90% confidence interval" has been from minus 25.71% to plus 41.06%. That means that 90% of the time, one year returns will fall in that range. That's a huge range and, as I mentioned above, the range can be even greater.

The lesson? Stock market returns can vary widely over the short term. Over five-year and ten-year periods, the range of returns is much tighter and more predictable.

So remember folks—this is where your long-term money goes, **not** the renovation fund or cash reserves.

In the years when equities outperformed, however, they outperformed by a huge margin and that's why the long-term returns of equities are the best.

The message here is that your asset mix should be based on YOUR situation, taking into consideration the following factors:

1. **Time horizon**—How long before the invested capital will be needed?
2. **Your need for liquidity.** Always set aside adequate money for any planned lump sum expenditures (cars or vacations) or emergencies, for at least two years.
3. **Your need for income from the portfolio**. If you are still working with no plans to retire, this need may be nil, but if you depend on the portfolio for your monthly income, this need might be high.
4. **Your risk tolerance**. This is both psychological and financial. If you have a large portfolio and your annual income far exceeds your expenses, you can afford to have a more aggressive portfolio (more in equities), because you can allow for the time needed to smooth out the returns.

When you combine a proper asset allocation for your situation with intelligent diversification, you go a long way toward minimizing the actual risk in your portfolio.

34

Can You Time the Stock Market?

IT HAS BEEN A LOUSY DECADE on the stock markets, but many investors have still managed to earn very attractive returns over that time. How come?

I say "lousy" compared to the longer term averages. For context, the Toronto S&P TSX Composite Index provided average total annual returns of 1.7% for the five-year period ending March 31, 2012. This includes dividends received. The American S&P 500 (large US companies) returned 2%, when measured in US dollars, ignoring currency effects.

The 20-year averages are closer to 9%.

So, here's a pop quiz for you... *When recent averages are less than the historical long-term averages, is this likely to be an attractive time to invest, or a less attractive time?*

Here's some more information—from April 1, 2009 to March 31, 2012, the three-year S&P TSX return was 15.6%. Not bad. However, the one-year return to March 31, 2012 was negative 9.8%.

The three-month return to that March 31 was positive 3.66%, but the market dropped over 3% in the following two weeks.

So, were any of those points in time particularly good times to invest? Any suggest bad times?

Here's another question... Why does the average mutual fund investor earn less than the average return of the fund in which he or she invests?

It's because many investors buy when the markets are high and sell when the markets are low, basing their decisions on headlines, economic forecasts and their personal outlook on the future. Call it buying on optimism and selling on pessimism.

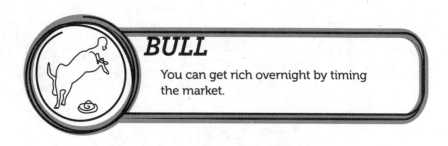

BULL

You can get rich overnight by timing the market.

The market on which shares trade every day—what we call "the stock market"—is subject to moods, based on its collective outlook for the future. When the mood is pessimistic, stock prices are low, usually a better time to buy. "Low" in this case means that you pay less—on average—for each dollar of earnings for the average company.

The cost of a dollar of earnings is called the **price to earnings ratio**, or **PE**. If a share is trading at $10 and the company's current profits are one dollar per share, then that company is trading at a PE of 10. If shares are trading at $20 for every dollar of profit, then the PE is 20 for that company.

Investors are willing to pay a higher PE for companies they expect to grow, and lower for ones they don't expect to grow, or when they expect profits to actually fall.

Across the market average, the PE multiple is a measure of the market's outlook for the market and the economy in general. When there is too much optimism—think of 1999 and 2007—you have to pay too much for stocks.

When there is "blood in the streets," as there was at the end of 2008 and the first few months of 2009, and stocks are dirt cheap, it is because everyone is afraid of them. Interestingly, if you had invested in the S&P TSX index at the time of maximum pessimism on March 1, 2009, **you made a profit of about 50% over the subsequent 12 months.**

This is largely thanks to a phenomenon called *PE multiple expansion*. That's a fancy name for saying that the fearful market was only willing to pay, say, seven dollars for a dollar of earnings in March, 2009, and 12 months later growing optimism encouraged the market to pay an expanding multiple, say, $12 for a dollar of earnings. That PE ratio expansion meant that, on average, company share prices might have doubled, even if their profits had only increased slightly.

This was based on fear flowing out of the market, and some measure of optimism returning. It was the *outlook* that had changed, much more than the economic fundamentals.

This is a rising tide that lifts all boats, and can result in big increases in share prices. What if you pick companies that are also increasing their profits? Over time, the market rewards good companies more than mediocre ones, so picking the right companies generally means more price stability in times of pessimism, and a bigger increase when optimism also results in PE expansion.

OK, so here's your homework:

Find out the current PE ratio, either for a certain stock market index or for an individual company stock in which you are interested. Compare that to the long-term average PE ratio for that market index or company, and think about whether or not right now is an attractive time to invest, or a less attractive time. Be prepared to defend your answer. ☺

But what about the Investment Planning Process?

I'm glad you asked; that means you have been listening.

There would appear to be a contradiction between what I said about the great opportunities available when the stock market is filled with fear, and the strategic investment planning approach, which ignores the markets and the economy and bases your actions on your own situation.

That strategic approach and the Investment Planning Process both suggest that the right time to invest in stocks or equities is when you personally need to increase the equity allocation in your portfolio. This need is based on re-balancing back toward your personal target asset mix.

Therefore, the decision about whether to invest now or not is entirely dependent on your situation, and whether or not your long-term portfolio needs an increase in its equity weighting. This has absolutely nothing to do with what is the current PE ratio of the market.

So, how do we reconcile these two positions? Simply remember that re-balancing your portfolio back toward your target asset allocation every three months will automatically mean buying more stocks after they have gone down, and selling them after they have gone up more quickly than the other asset classes. This means you will take advantage of those market mood swings, without having to guess which way the market is going or if you are at the top or the bottom.

The truth is that you cannot predict the direction of the market. You can't predict when a pessimistic market is going to turn around and start to become more optimistic, expanding PEs. You can't predict when the optimistic market is going to suffer a correction, even when it is valued way above its long-term averages.

So, the lesson is to invest according to your personal cash needs and resources, your goals, risk tolerance and the other factors described in the Investment Planning Process.

So why the homework question? Investors are still wise to pay attention to the current PE ratio of the market compared to its long-term averages. It contributes to your long-term experience and instincts about the markets. After a while, you will become better at sensing when the market is undervalued, and being able to buy good quality companies at your target price. This is subtly different than trying to time the market. I would call this taking advantage of other people's fear. We encourage that.

35

A Critical Word
About Fluctuation

IF AT ANY TIME you become overly optimistic or relaxed about your investments, take that opportunity to remind yourself that equity investments can fluctuate. As Louis Rukeyser once said, "Sometimes they fluck down; sometimes they fluck up."[13]

Are you prepared to withstand these fluctuations, financially and psychologically?

To repeat the most important part of investment planning, your personal asset mix should have nothing to do with whether the markets are high or low, or whether the "consensus" of the years gloomy or giddy. Both will be wrong before long.

Predictions and opinions about the future are a dime a dozen—just turn on the TV or surf to any investor website to prove this. Halfway through a long day of writing this book, I had to make a quick trip to the chiropractor's office. The waiting room had several copies of the magazine *Canadian Business* on the shelf. One month's cover story told me I would never be able to retire, while two months later there was an optimistic photo of a man in bathing trunks jumping in the air accompanying the title, "Retire happy!"

On their website today is a headline saying, "Greek ETF up sharply but still too much risk." What the hell does that mean?

And *Canadian Business* is one of the more balanced publications out there. The TV shows and website articles and ads scare the pants off me.

No, you can't depend on the financial media for investment decisions. Instead, your personal mixture of equities, bonds and short-term investments is based

---

[13]   Louis Rukeyser, *Wall Street Week*, long-running US Public TV show on investing.

on your unique situation. Your need for liquidity over the next two to three years should be met with guaranteed investments that are liquid or will mature when you need them. These investments also benefit from rising interest rates, generally negative for stocks and bonds.

Your requirement for income from the portfolio (if any) should be met by interest paid on bonds, debentures and other fixed income investments, by reliable dividends on high-quality blue chip stocks, and other cash distributions from reliable investments. This will have a bearing on how much of your portfolio needs to be in fixed income or bond-like investments (which can still fluctuate in value).

Your time horizon is important, as is your rate of savings or withdrawals. All of these factors make up your financial ability to tolerate short-term fluctuation and risk.

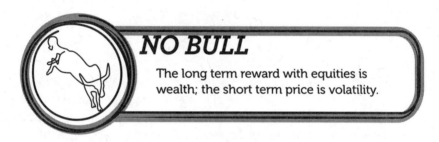

NO BULL
The long term reward with equities is wealth; the short term price is volatility.

Perhaps most important is your psychological risk tolerance. If you cashed in everything in 2008 because you couldn't stand to see your investments decline any more, only to go back into the stock markets in the last few years after a period of sustained growth, you would be wise to measure your current exposure to equities and sit down with an advisor who can tell you if you have an appropriate asset mix.

If you are going to sell again at the bottom of the next bear market and you are over-exposed to equities for your personal situation, now is the time to make a change.

On the other hand, if you are able to ignore the day-to-day fluctuations and the occasional year of negative returns, confident that the balance in your portfolio will provide components that rise at the same time that others fall, then your current asset mix is likely appropriate and does not need changes.

Here is a summary of what I believe:

- Stock market returns vary greatly from year to year;
- In the long run (most 5-year and almost all 10-year periods), stocks outperform bonds and treasury bills;
- Stock prices fluctuate significantly in the shorter term, as you know, so there

is substantial capital risk if you invest for short periods of time.
- When the stock market has just had a terrible year (and everyone is predicting lower returns going forward), you will earn more in the next five years than if the market has just gone up for two or three years in a row (when everyone is predicting continued happy days). How 'bout that?

36

Diversifying Your Diversification

IN THIS CHAPTER we will go into more detail about how proper diversification can protect your portfolio.

We started up this investing section of the book with a wonderful quote from the American writer Will Rogers. About stock market investing, he famously said, *"Don't gamble. Take all your savings and buy a good stock, and hold it till it goes up, then sell it. If it don't go up, don't buy it."*

Thanks, Will. That's very helpful—sort of like describing golf as a "simple game." Just hit the ball into the hole.

As investors and golfers both know, such simple ideas are sometimes difficult to execute, especially when the market or the golf course refuses to cooperate.

So, how do you remove more of the element of chance from your investing? How do you make sure that your portfolio earns something in almost all weather conditions and suffers the least amount of damage when a hurricane hits?

The one word answer is **diversification**, usually focused on avoiding large short-term fluctuations in the portfolio. This means putting money into fixed income investments like bonds and GICs, short-term investments like treasury bills or high interest savings accounts, as well as putting money in shares of companies, which is a necessity for long-term wealth creation.

Although fixed income and short-term investments provide lower returns over a full market cycle and are less tax efficient than equities, they are a necessary balance for most people. They provide the liquidity, income and stability that most people require.

But how do you go beyond that, to provide more consistent positive returns?

For most people, real estate is the next asset class to use. Houses, cottages and investment real estate all qualify, although for investment purposes, we focus on the real estate that you don't—and won't—live in. These are properties you may sell down the road and not replace with another residence, and which provide you with current and future income that you can spend and live on.

The ideal vehicles for investment real estate, especially to start, are vehicles with liquidity, as opposed to your personal direct ownership in real estate rental properties. Real estate investment trusts (REITs) and real estate mutual funds are likely the best place for you to start. These can generally be sold at any time, unlike a property you own. As well, they don't take any of your time to manage, maintain or collect rents.

If your investment account allows it, consider purchasing an index of REITs, like XRE. This allows you to diversify across all real estate investment sectors, including apartments, warehouses, shopping centres, hotels and even seniors homes, with one flexible investment period

Hedge funds or "alternative investments" can be another way to diversify beyond the traditional asset classes. Many sophisticated investors have begun using hedge funds over the last 10 years, but unfortunately the term "hedge fund" has become meaningless, because now it is applied to all manner of investment strategies and vehicles, with the only common thread being that they are less regulated than conventional mutual funds.

A "hedge" should mean a counterbalancing investment to decrease risk, where an investment is made that will generally go up when others go down. Think of betting on both red and black in roulette. Unfortunately, some hedge funds place big bets on one colour, and often get burned.

Interestingly, the US dollar has proven to be a very effective hedge over the last five years, because every time there is a panic over banking system liquidity, sovereign debt or future recessions, the US dollar has risen while most other financial assets have declined.

We always make sure that our clients have investments in oil companies, because rising oil prices will mean higher profits for those companies, while, at the same time, the clients are paying more to fill up their gas tanks. That seems to me to be a classic hedge.

The more useful terms than "hedge fund" are "alternative investments" or especially "absolute return," which describes a fund that sets out to make a small amount of money each month no matter what the market conditions. A manager does this by using as many as 14 strategies like long-short (buying some stocks and selling others that he doesn't own, with the expectation that those ones will go down and he can buy them back later), asset-backed lending, arbitrage, event-driven, distressed securities, etc.

We won't explain how all of these work here, as that would take many chapters. This knowledge would only be worthwhile if you intend to be your own investment manager. But most important for you to know is that you need to be cautious with these investments, as it appears that some of the managers of these funds don't know what they are doing, either.

Private equity (usually buying shares or convertible debt of companies that do not yet trade on a stock market) can be another way to achieve high returns that are not directly correlated to the stock market. Typically, this requires big money to get involved with the sophisticated managers who have access to the best opportunities.

A colleague of mine in Victoria regularly sends me the Yale University Endowment Fund annual report, useful because this fund has achieved returns that far exceed those of most large portfolios. Here was the target asset mix for their long term fund, in 2008:

Absolute Return	25%
Domestic (US) Equity	12%
Fixed Income	4%
Foreign Equity (incl. Canada)	15%
Private Equity	17%
Real Assets	27%
Cash	(none, as it is held in a separate account for funding and liquidity needs)

Is this a practical mix for you? Likely not, as Yale has $18 billion to work with, and a team of academics who teach and develop investment theory full-time, in addition to multiple teams of outside managers. For example, "real assets" mentioned above include things like toll bridges and roads, power plans and other reliable income producing vehicles, which require billions to purchase or invest in.

As well, this mix includes only their long-term funds, and not the separate funding accounts that the endowment fund uses to provide for their annual withdrawal requirements.

However, you can use this sample asset mix as a guide to expand your thinking (and that of your investment advisor) to beyond just the traditional cash, fixed income and equities.

In practical terms for your portfolio, strive to diversify properly within each of your asset classes, and definitely add real estate as a distinct asset class, tracking it separately from your other equities.

37

Make Your Wealth Accumulation Automatic (and Beat the Herd)

ONE THING you absolutely have to do is make your wealth accumulation plan automatic. No one can always remember to write that monthly cheque to the mutual fund company or consistently choose investing over that new pair of shoes or spontaneous trip to Vegas with your best friends.

What works perfectly to make it automatic? Payroll deduction.

Think about the one huge bill that ALWAYS gets paid. Give up?

How about your income taxes... the government figured out decades ago that they didn't want to wait till the end of the year to get their cash, and they certainly didn't want to depend on Canadian taxpayers to be disciplined enough to set aside 30% of their paycheques every two weeks and leave the money untouched until needed April 30. They worried that would not happen, in way too many cases.

And you know what? They're right.

So the government made it a law that they get paid first. You can make it your law that you get paid first, right after them.

Ideally, you will pay yourself with pre-tax dollars. We talked about how to do that by setting up a regular pre-authorized cheque plan into an RRSP, and then decreasing your income tax withholding at source to give you more money to invest. If your employer has any type of savings or retirement plan into which they match your contributions, this is obviously even better. If you can turn your $100 a month into $200 per month by using the company's money, then you get to your goal in half the time.

So how do you beat the market?

There are two ways to almost guarantee it.

The first is to do what we've already described—invest a fixed amount of money regularly for a sustained period of time. By investing in a fluctuating investment like an equity mutual fund, your fixed amount of dollars automatically purchase more of the investment when the price is low, and less when the price is high.

For example, when you invest $100 into a mutual fund with a unit value of $10 per unit, you automatically purchase 10 units per month. If the unit value goes up to $11, then your next $100 investment will only purchase 9.1 units.

Let's say that in the third month there is a significant market correction, and the unit value drops to $9 per unit. In that month your smart money will automatically purchase 11.1 units, stocking up while the price is low.

At first blush, this would appear to work out evenly, but let's do the math to make sure. After three months, your $300 has purchased 30.2 units. When the price returns to $10 per unit, your investment is already worth $302, a gain of two thirds of 1%, even though the market itself shows no gains. The longer the markets stay low while you are accumulating, the better. If we had six months of the fund at $9 and then an increase back to $10, the return would be more like 11%.

This example may turn you into a fan of bad markets! With my own personal investments, I don't mind a sustained period of declining stock prices, since I am investing regularly every month. I know that the longer the market stays low, the better the prices I am paying for the investments I want. I do not plan on drawing on the money for several years, and even then I plan to just live on the dividends. That gives many years for the prices to recover.

The other way to consistently beat the market is by regularly re-balancing your portfolio back toward your target asset mix. This also guarantees that you will "buy low and sell high" more often.

Setting up a framework of regular re-balancing also overcomes the long list of human and psychological factors that often stand in the way of investment success.

When it comes to changing market conditions and economic climate, I encourage you to *respond*, and not just *react*. This means respond *thoughtfully*—as opposed to *impulsively*—to changing factors. Try to focus on changes in your own situation, more than the world. The forces that drive things out in the world will eventually return to their long-term patterns, often when least expected. If you are always reacting, it will usually be at the wrong time.

Example—the market crash of 2008 scared everyone, me included. That was natural, as it was a very scary time. It would be easy now, several years later, to say we should have all been calm back then and realized that the time of maximum panic was an historic buying opportunity.

But it was not easy or natural, in late 2008 and early 2009, to calmly do what the text books say to do. The impulse was to run, by selling everything. Instead, taking advantage of bargain prices by buying falling stocks, real estate investment trusts or even corporate bonds and preferred shares required that you had in place a system that you trusted, and the ability to say, "My strategy was designed for times like this—I have to trust the system, now more than ever."

That strategy is to have a written Investment Policy Statement (IPS) that specifies the target percentage of your portfolio that will be in short term guaranteed investments, fixed income investments, and equities in Canada, the US and the rest of the world.

You then re-balance the portfolio quarterly (or even monthly) so that the actual asset mix is measured and adjusted back toward the target. This means when the stock market has crashed and bonds have gone up, you will automatically sell some bonds and buy some stocks. This ensures a measure of selling high and buying low.

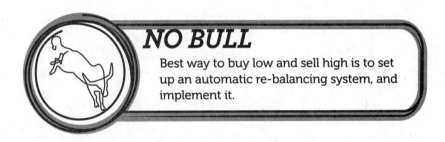

NO BULL

Best way to buy low and sell high is to set up an automatic re-balancing system, and implement it.

It's easy, other than requiring discipline, consistency and reasonably low trading costs, along with your trust in the system when a really tough environment like 2008 comes along.

In 2008, as the market fell, this system required additional amounts of money to be moved into equities as the stock portion of the portfolio fell. For six months or more, as the market fall accelerated, this looked like a bad strategy. However, as has always happened, it kept the asset mix appropriate for the investor's situation, and it kept the portfolio prepared for the recovery.

"Buy low; sell high"

Guess what—that's hard to do in real life. The system we have described automatically makes it happen, most valuably at times when most of us would be reacting to fear, and refusing to buy.

To buy something when it is actually low—*priced at less than its true value*—means that you actually have to buy when others are scared and when the asset you are buying is out of favour. This may be a time when the "smartest" investors in the world are running from the market.

To sell high, you have to be willing to sell a stock that has been your loyal friend, a stock that has made you money, and a stock that everyone else is saying has a beautiful future. In practice, it often means reducing your exposure to stocks in general, just when other investors are most optimistic about the stock market.

NO BULL
Selling high can mean saying goodbye to some favourite stocks.

Most of us can't consistently do that on our own, so we need a system that helps us do it. A lot of us also need an outside advisor, to make sure we stick to our system.

As financial advisors, we also have to trust the system, but some of our professional value is to exercise independent judgment as to how (and when) the system is implemented.

In 2008, for example, we delayed our client stock purchases and re-balancing (even talking a few enthusiastic clients out of going "all in" too soon), as we could see that the bottom had not been reached. By holding off and then adding more to equities near the actual market bottom, we made the system work better.

But I cannot consistently predict the future, nor can you or your advisor. In 2008, we could have been wrong, and the recovery could have started sooner than we expected, causing us to miss out on some of that powerful early growth of the market.

We advisors also have to overcome our human limitations by trusting the system of target asset mix and consistent, regular re-balancing, paying close attention to the cash and liquidity needs of the family.

By always having a cash reserve, paying attention to your future cash needs and always having enough money in guaranteed investments, you can avoid ever being forced into selling low.

Remember that your target asset mix may have to be changed very quickly if *your* situation changes, through things like starting a family, losing your job, approaching retirement, or buying a house.

Remember, your target asset mix is all about you, and your current situation, not about the markets or the economy.

38

Choosing the Right Tool to Ride the Bull

Mutual funds and ETFs

Many people have portfolios that are too small to make it practical to use individual stocks. Other people would rather have a professional manager pick the shares in their portfolio.

Mutual funds are a great solution for such investors, and especially for people beginning their investment experience. Different mutual funds invest in different asset classes, so some only own stocks, bonds, or short term guaranteed investments, or a mixture of several asset classes. In this chapter, we are going to focus on funds that invest only in stocks.

When you invest in a mutual fund, you become part of a pool of investors set up by that fund company, to use a full-time, professional manager to choose the investments. The fund collects the dividends and the cash from sales of investments when the manager chooses to sell.

The mutual fund is sort of a "co-op" approach to investing. Some of the advantages include guaranteed daily liquidity at the closing price each trading day, the ability to invest small amounts, as little as $50 per month, and the ease of administration. The mutual fund takes care of all those things, and provides a single comprehensive tax slip at the end of each year.

There are actually different structures of mutual funds.

In a mutual fund trust, you own units of the fund, and become a unit holder. The net taxable income of the fund is allocated 100% to the unit holders each year.

In a mutual fund corporation (often referred to in marketing material as "capital class"), you own **shares** of a **corporation**, instead of units of the trust. The corporation has more tax flexibility to defer tax, and is not required to distribute this taxable income to the shareholders each year.

Both of these structures are "open-ended funds" where the fund agrees to buy back your units at the end of every trading day, at the net asset value per unit or per share.

There are also types of "closed-end funds," where either the units or the shares trade between investors during the trading day. In this case, the managers do not guarantee to buy back your investment at all, and instead you need to find another buyer.

When you invest in an ETF (exchange traded fund), you are buying shares of the ETF from other sellers during the trading day, just like any other share. The difference between an ETF and an active business company is that the only assets of the ETF are a basket of shares (or bonds), usually replicating a recognized index of shares (or bonds). Management fees for such passive (index tracking) ETFs are generally much lower than for the active management approach of most mutual funds.

An example of an index is the S&P TSX Composite Index, made up of the largest 200 or so stocks trading on the Toronto Stock Exchange. A sub index, which you can also purchase through an ETF, might be an ETF investing only in energy companies, only real estate investment trusts or only financial stocks. The ETF's collect dividends from the underlying stocks and, in many cases, offer to distribute them to you, the investor, or to reinvest them. In this way, they are similar to a mutual fund.

Most mutual funds are actively managed, which means the manager conducts research and uses judgment as to when to purchase or dispose of stocks and other investments. Most ETF's are passively managed, which means they simply track an index. In this case, there is no discrimination between the profitability of each company making up the index, or the price being paid for a dollar of each company's profit.

Common sense would suggest that a professional manager should be able to perform better than a passive index, which lumps mediocre companies in with good ones. However, research shows that far fewer than half of professional mutual

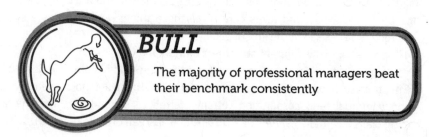

BULL

The majority of professional managers beat their benchmark consistently fund managers consistently outperform their respective benchmark index over a longer period of time.

Most research also shows that the managers tend to lag the index by roughly the amount of the management fees and expenses of running the fund. Mutual funds have a management expense ratio (MER), made up of the management fees, GST or HST on that fee, plus accounting and mailing costs and other expenses. Most retail mutual funds also pay an ongoing commission or service fee to the investment advisor who administers the account. When all of this is added together, it exceeds 2% for most retail mutual funds, and can reach 3% or even more for specialty funds or high-cost providers.

Part of the management fee is paid back to the mutual fund dealer who sponsors the financial advisor. This is usually called a trailer commission, which is a form of service fee. The amount typically ranges from 0.5% per year for bond funds, and up to 1% per year for equity funds.

You can also choose to have your advisor paid an upfront fee, in exchange for agreeing to a financial plan or providing advice. This commission fee is usually paid by the mutual fund company to the dealer and advisor in the form of a Deferred Sales Charge, or DSC. The fund company earns this fee back over time through the management fees. However, if you withdraw from that fund company before it has had time to earn all of this fee back, the fund company charges the remaining portion to you as a redemption fee; hence the name "deferred sales charge."

There are low-cost mutual fund companies like Steadyhand Funds, with whom people can invest directly, without the use of a financial advisor or licensed salesperson. There are no commissions of any kind involved here, hence the management fees can be much less.

There are also advisor funds called "F-Class" funds, which have unbundled the management fees and commissions, and do not pay your advisor. This reduces the costs by as much as 1%. However, to access F-Class funds, an investor typically needs to pay fees directly to their advisor. Such an account is typically called a "fee-based" account.

More on Exchange Traded Funds

ETFs generally have much lower ongoing costs than mutual funds. The ETFs that invest in large mainstream indices (as opposed to specialty or foreign indices) cost as little as 0.25% to 0.4% per year in management costs. However, a commission is paid to buy and sell them. The amount you pay in commission will depend on whether your account is with a discount broker or a full-service investment dealer.

Exchange traded funds are a great tool. We use them all the time in our investment management practice, and have for a number of years. For many uses, I prefer them to conventional retail mutual funds.

They became popular for a number of good reasons. An ETF allows you convenient access to a basket of stocks (or other investments) with one purchase. That single stock or unit can be bought and sold on the stock market at any time during the trading day.

The basket of underlying investments is usually selected based on pre-set and transparent criteria (like the TSX 60 index, for example, which is published daily), so you can always know what you own.

I contrast this with an actively-managed mutual fund, where the manager has to delay release of his exact portfolio, to keep trade secrets and keep competitors from stealing ideas.

Another contrast with mutual funds is the fees. Traditionally, ETFs have charged between .3% and .5% per year for access to a passive index, while the average actively-managed fund costs more like 2% to 2.5% per year, including advisor compensation (or about 1% less without advisor compensation). Some cost more; a few cost less.

Index-based ETFs are also usually low turnover vehicles, and therefore quite tax-efficient.

There continues an active debate about the relative merits of active and passive management, with no clear winner. Either tool can help you reach your financial goals.

No matter what your approach, remember that making an equity investment means becoming an owner of companies, with all of the rewards and risks of ownership. The rewards can be great, but the short-term cost is almost always volatility.

39

Deposit Insurance— Keep Your Protection Clear

IN JANUARY, 2007, Ralph invested $90,000 into a mutual fund at his favourite bank. In March, 2009, after the stock market correction, the fund was worth $63,453.

Ralph wasn't worried, as he assumed (incorrectly) that he had $100,000 of deposit insurance guarantee on that money, and asked the bank for his $90,000 back.

I won't say they laughed, but....

People often ask me about deposit insurance, but in the same breath ask me how safe is a certain stock or bond market investment they are about to make. It is important to be clear—**there is no deposit insurance on fluctuating investments**.

"Deposits" in banks, credit unions and investment dealers are guaranteed and insured against loss, within certain limits. However, many "investments" (like mutual funds) made through those same institutions are subject to fluctuations in value due to market conditions, so the original principal is not guaranteed.

To get such a guarantee on a mutual fund investment, one must purchase a "segregated fund" through a life insurance company, and pay a higher management expense ratio for the guarantee. As well, the guarantee only pays out on the death of the account holder, or at the end of a 10-year period following the last guarantee reset value.

Money invested through investment dealers, is protected against dealer insolvency—more on that in a moment—but not against market fluctuations.

This may be a little confusing, but don't worry; confusion is step one in opening your mind to new information.

A "deposit" is money you *loan* to a financial institution, by opening up a chequing or savings account, or purchasing a GIC. The institution's part of the agreement is to pay you back, either on your demand (with a chequing or savings account) or at the agreed maturity date, in the case of a GIC or term deposit.

Such deposits at banks are guaranteed for up to $100,000 per depositor by the Canada Deposit Insurance Corporation (CDIC), a Crown corporation created by Parliament. This covers Canadian dollar deposits (not US dollar accounts), plus GICs of up to five years, money orders, travellers' cheques and bank drafts, and deposit-type investments in RRSPs, RRIFs and TFSAs.

A single person or a family can enjoy much more than $100,000 in coverage, because each of the following qualifies as a separate "depositor":

- one name
- joint name
- in trust for another person
- RRSP
- RRIF
- TFSA
- property tax account for mortgaged property

Know the rules before you assume you have more protection than you really do, by visiting www.cdic.ca/ and reading the rules, or by phoning 1-800-461-2342 with questions.

At investment dealers, the Canadian Investor Protection Fund covers up to $1 million per "customer," but combines the accounts held by one person, either directly or indirectly.

This only covers losses from the insolvency of an investment dealer, and includes loss of securities, certificates, commodities and futures contracts, and cash. However, typically, another investment dealer or financial institution would take over these accounts and guarantee them to the customers, instead.

With mutual fund dealers and mutual fund managers, your funds are usually held separate from the assets of those companies, so even a bankruptcy or other failure of the fund dealer or fund company should not result in the loss of any of your investment value. Another company would produce the management contracts, or be assigned to look after these funds, either on an ongoing basis or until they can be liquidated.

However, the value of any fluctuating investment fund will continue to fluctuate, period; this means that even though your investment is protected in such circumstances, a 10% decline in the market in which your fund is invested will still likely result in a 10% decrease in the value of your particular investment fund.

The easy way to remember all this is that deposit insurance only covers depositors—people who have loaned their money to a financial institution, in exchange for a guaranteed return and a guaranteed return of capital.

On the other hand, investors have become owners of the investments they make, with all the risks and uncertainties that come with being an owner. This includes mutual funds that invest in fluctuating investments, even if those mutual funds are purchased through a bank, credit union or other institution whose deposits are covered by deposit insurance.

Managing the Bull:
Detect and Deflect the Crap

SUCCESSFUL INVESTING is a long term undertaking, so it naturally takes patience. Patience is needed to stick with a plan for years or decades, until compound growth can really do its magic. As well, shorter-term patience is needed when the economic cycles or market corrections work against you, and temporarily make your strategy look wrong.

Courage may also be important. Often, courage is needed to buy equities when the markets are falling and the news is bad. The most successful investors are the ones who can buy equities or other fallen investments when there is "blood in the streets" and more timid investors are running for the exit.

Courage may also be needed when it's time to sell some equities when the markets are very high and appear bound to rise higher, in order to re-balance a portfolio back to its target asset mix.

Successful investors are good at controlling their emotions of fear and greed, and preventing these emotions from pushing them off their long-term plan. Such investors may be intuitive, but they do not act prematurely on the impulses that emanate from high emotions.

The way that ALL investors can achieve such success is to put in place a framework that overrides emotion, and enforces patience and courage by replacing them with a systematic re-balancing strategy.

This is called the Investment Planning Process.

To be successful, an investor will:

1. follow the Investment Planning Process,
2. keep emotions (either positive or negative) from causing detours from the set strategy, and
3. stay out of the way while the investment plan and the chosen vehicles do their jobs.

Proper planning and time will lead to success.

Part 5

Working the Bull:
Reducing Your Tax Burden

Let me tell you how it will be,
there's one for you, 19 for me...:
'cause I'm the Taxman

     – GEORGE HARRISON, 1966

40

The "Three Ds" of Tax Planning

INCOME AND OTHER TAXES will be your single largest expenditure over the course of your working life. We want to help you reduce the amount of income taxes you pay—now and in retirement—so we have devoted several chapters to helping you understand how the tax system works, and how you can make it work better for you.

If you sophisticated readers will bear with me for a minute, I want to review the basics of how the income tax system works. This may be a great chapter to pass onto your kids or friends to read, if it's all old hat to you.

Canadian income tax is based on residency, not citizenship. We pay income tax on a figure called taxable income, which is made up of a number of different types of income.

Types of taxable income include employment income, net self-employment income, net rental income, interest income, 50% of the gain or profit on the sale of capital property, pension income, RRSP or RRIF withdrawals and other forms of net business or professional income, including things like royalties.

Dividend income is money you receive from a corporation in which you are a shareholder, when that corporation declares dividends. Through a complicated calculation of gross up and dividend tax credit, the rate you pay on one dollar of dividend is less than for a dollar of income from any of the sources mentioned above. That acknowledges the fact that the corporation had to pay tax before it could pay you a dividend and the system tries to avoid double taxation. This will become important when we talk about investment strategy.

Canada has a "progressive tax system." This means that as your taxable income increases, the tax rate becomes progressively higher and higher. These tax rates are lumped together in "brackets." For example, Manitoba has a tax bracket that applies to taxable incomes between $31,000 and $42,707, with a marginal tax rate (MTR) of 27%, and another bracket that runs from $42,708 to $67,000, with a marginal tax rate of 35%.

Since the federal tax brackets change annually with inflation and tax rates can change with federal or provincial budgets, we are rounding off and reminding you that the rates are different from province to province.

The MTR refers to the percent tax charged on the next dollar of income. So, if my taxable income is $50,000 and I earn $1,000 of interest income on top of that, the interest would be taxed at 35% in our example, or $350 of tax on that $1,000 of interest.

The same rate works in reverse if you have a deduction (not a credit) from taxable income. For example, if I have $50,000 of taxable income, then $1,000 contributed to an RRSP will reduce my tax by $350.

Roughly the first $10,000 of income each year is tax free under something they call the basic personal amount. This is an important planning tool, as every individual from the time they are born is eligible for this amount. If your two-year old is paid $8,000 to star in a television commercial, make sure the child is paid rather than you, as the income will be legitimately tax free.

Before you get too excited, the CRA enforces a group of rules in the Income Tax Act loosely referred to as the attribution rules, which make it either difficult or impossible to arbitrarily allocate income from your tax return to a family member who has little or no income.

A good way to start thinking about reducing income taxes is to remember the "Three Ds":
1. Deduct
2. Defer
3. Divide
   (No, not "deny;" that will get you in trouble.)

You want to take all of the **deductions** for which you are eligible or can arrange to make eligible, you want to **defer** income into the future where possible, and you want to **divide** income among family members, so that tax is paid at the lowest possible rate.

As you prepare your tax return (or carefully go over your professionally-prepared return line by line), pay close attention to the items that resulted in additional tax beyond that calculated on your salary.

Did you have interest, dividends, or capital gains? Did you have employment bonuses? Commissions?

In terms of deductions, did you use RRSP or pension contributions, carrying charges, or other investment expenses to reduce your taxable income?

A fourth "D" in tax planning could be to **Define**, which means to become clear on the tax rules and how they affect your personal situation.

Let's look first at decreasing taxes. Investment income is one of the areas where you have the most flexibility. If you pay tax on interest income, you have an opportunity here, as you might be able to convert that income to dividends or capital gains. Interest is taxed at the highest marginal tax rate on which you personally pay tax. That could be 27% to 44% or even higher, depending on your province of residence and your income.

Dividends are taxed at much lower rates. In fact, "eligible" dividends enjoy a *negative* tax rate in many provinces, for taxpayers in the first tax bracket. This means that a person earning less than about $38,000 of taxable income can actually receive a dividend and the net tax credit on top of that.

Eligible dividends are those paid out to you by public companies that have already paid corporate tax at the high rate. The tax system wants to avoid double taxation at the highest personal tax rate, and this computes to be very low tax in the lower tax brackets.

If you can earn the same dollars in dividends as you can in interest, you're a long way ahead with dividends. Even if the dividends are slightly lower, there is often going to be a net benefit. You earn dividends by owning shares in a corporation that pays dividends, or a mutual fund that invests in shares of such corporations and flows the dividends through to you. (Remember, all of this applies to investments held outside registered accounts, not in your RRSP or TFSA.)

The second potential benefit of owning common shares is that, over time, they will usually increase in value, as the company's profits and dividends grow. As long as you continue to own the shares, they can double or triple in value with no tax payable on the growth. You only pay tax when you actually sell the shares, and then you only pay tax on half of the gain.

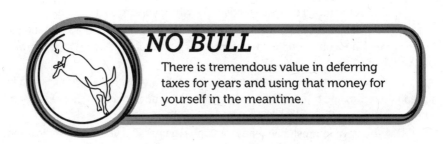

NO BULL

There is tremendous value in deferring taxes for years and using that money for yourself in the meantime.

Of course, putting any investments inside a TFSA shelters all investment income from tax. As well, there is no tax when you take the money out of the TFSA, no matter how much it has grown. This eliminates tax completely on that investment income. That's goal number one.

Placing your money inside an RRSP and then making your investments in that account defers the tax until a future withdrawal, which is a close second in value.

Deduct

Another way to reduce your taxes is to create deductions. Maximizing your RRSP contributions is the easiest way, but once you have done that, what do you do?

Some people borrow money to invest outside of their RRSP, because the interest on the loan is a deduction from taxable income.

RRSP contributions, deductible interest, investment counsel fees and other carrying charges all reduce your taxable income and save you tax at your marginal tax rate.

Defer

Ways to defer taxes include removing investment income from your tax return. (No, I don't mean hiding it.) This is done by earning investment income inside an RRSP, inside a tax-exempt life insurance policy or by owning investments that gradually go up in value while you continue to own them. This generates a capital gain, which only has to be claimed when you sell the investment. This is one of the advantages of owning mutual funds or stocks.

The benefit of deferral is that you get to use the money for a longer period of time. If the Finance Minister said "I know you owe me $100, but why don't you pay me back in 2040?" that would be a pretty good offer, wouldn't it?

The simplest way to defer tax on investment income is the use of RRSP's. The deferral can continue on into your retirement, and the total tax does not have to be paid until the death of the second spouse.

Outside the RRSP, buying and holding stocks or tax-efficient mutual funds can be an excellent way to defer tax on investment income. Keep in mind, though, when the manager sells stocks within your mutual fund for a net gain, that gain does have to be distributed to you each year and claimed on your tax return.

As we have discussed in the protection area, tax-exempt, permanent life insurance also defers tax on investment earnings, and converts the deferred tax to a tax-free payout on death.

Divide

Make sure that all family members get use of the personal credit amount. Every person (no matter what their age) is allowed to earn roughly $10,000 of income tax-free. Unfortunately, it's not just as simple as transferring investment assets into the name of a family member with lower income. The Income Tax Act specifies that investment income earned on capital that is gifted to a spouse or to a minor child attributes back to the person who gave the gift. However, there are ways around this.

With spouses, a loan at CRA's prescribed rate (currently 1%), with interest actually paid each year, avoids attribution. In the case of children, interest and dividends earned on the gift attribute back to the donor, but capital gains do not attribute back. The capital gains can be claimed on the child's tax returns, so there's an obvious strategy.

Above all, remember that filing tax returns is fun, especially since the government started saying "Thank you for filing this return" on your Notice of Assessment.

41

Deductions and Credits: Reducing the Taxes You Pay

LET'S SEE IF WE CAN ACCOMPLISH that goal of reducing your income taxes. First, it's good to understand that there is a difference between a deduction and a credit.

Deductions reduce taxable income, and therefore save tax at your marginal tax rate. This means that a $1,000 deduction might save you $270 of tax, $350 of tax or $440 tax, depending on your tax bracket and your marginal tax rate. Tax rates vary from province to province, but in all cases increase as your taxable income rises.

Other tax reduction items create an actual tax credit. This saves everyone tax at the same rate, which (with the exception of donations and political contributions) is at the lowest tax bracket, roughly 27% combined federal and provincial in most provinces. These include the Pension Credit, the Age Credit (for people age 65 and better) and the Medical Expense Credit, to name a few. Most credits are non-refundable, which means they can only reduce tax down to zero. A few are refundable, which means they will actually send you a cheque, even if you are not paying any tax.

Investment expenses such as interest on loans taken out to invest in a business or an income-producing investment are deductible from taxable income.

Fees paid to an investment counsel firm, investment manager or investment custodian for investment advice on non-registered investments, rent on a safety deposit box to hold certificates or investments, and accounting fees for calculating investment or rental income can be claimed each year as a deduction from taxable income.

Business owners, self-employed or commissioned salespeople can accelerate deductible expenses by buying equipment prior to year end. On this list, include computers, software, vehicles, office supplies, as well as maintenance and repairs, legal and accounting fees, salaries and bonuses, and business or educational tuition and travel.

Computers and software are now fully deductible in the year of purchase, while furniture, equipment or vehicle purchases allow for a deduction of half of the full year depreciation for the year in which you purchase, even if you only own the property for a few weeks. (If you wait until January, you will still only be able to claim half the usual depreciation in that year, not as good a deal.)

If any of these items apply to you, consult your accounting professional or financial advisor.

Each fall, ask your investment advisor for a *realized* capital gains report for the year-to-date for all of your unregistered investments (those outside of RRSP, RRIF or TFSA). If you have net capital gains realized that year ("winners"), then look at opportunities to sell securities that have declined in value since their initial purchase ("losers"), in order to realize the capital loss on the losers and offset those current-year gains.

Confirm that the Adjusted Cost Base (ACB) or book value shown on your statement is accurate and can be depended upon, and sell before December 24, for use in that year.

If you like the stock or fund, you can buy it back 31 days later. Re-purchasing any sooner will prevent you from using the claim for the loss, as CRA deems this a "superficial loss." An alternative is to immediately buy a similar security, one that is expected to have similar results in the future.

If you reported taxable capital gains in any of the last three tax years, you have an opportunity to recover the taxes you paid on those gains, by realizing overall net losses in the current year and carrying those losses back to the previous years. You do this by filing a T1A Request for Loss Carryback when you file your 2012 return.

Also look at gains in your TFSA, which you can realize tax-free. If you have significant unrealized gains, it may be worth realizing some profit and going to a more conservative investment, to lock in some of the profit. However, don't let the tax tail wag the investment dog—always look at the investment merits first, and just stay aware of the tax effects.

Similarly, if your children or grandchildren have "in-trust" accounts and they are earning less than $10,000 or so in total income, consider triggering capital gains on investments, on which they will pay no tax, and decrease their future taxable gain.

Give generously

Donations reduce your taxes by about 27% of the first $200 you donate each year, and 44% of all donations above that amount. December 31 is the contribution deadline.

If you are married, claim both spouses' receipts on one tax return, so that you maximize the higher rate credit on the amounts above $200 of donations per year.

If you donate stocks or mutual funds on which you have large gains directly to a charity "in-kind," then there is no tax on your capital gain. You will get the same 44% tax credit, so donate your investment "winners" instead of cash.

This is particularly effective with flow through shares. Getting a free ride on your flow through capital gain is even more important, as they have a zero cost for calculating capital gain. Therefore, half of the entire sale price is taxable, if sold on the open market. When donating, you eliminate the tax that would have otherwise been payable.

The most tax-effective gift is a political contribution, if you are so motivated. For donations up to $400 per year, tax credit rate is 75%. This means that a $400 political contribution reduces your actual taxes by $300, so the contribution only costs $100. On contributions between $400 and $750 in the same year, the tax credit is 50% of your contribution, reducing to 33⅓% for contributions between $750 and $1,275 in the same year.

NO BULL

Donating to charity—or to a political party—reduces tax by 44% to 75% of the donation.

These credits are "non-refundable," which means that they will only reduce tax otherwise payable, and not create a refund if you are not paying tax.

Be sure to claim the relatively new deductions and credits, like the Canada Employment Amount, Public Transit Pass Credit, Children's Fitness Amount, Children's Arts Tax Credit and tradesperson's tool deduction.

Other deductible expenses include your professional or union dues, possibly alimony or maintenance payments (depending on the date of your separation agreement), and any 2012 moving expenses.

Check the moving expense rules carefully. You might also have last year's moving expenses to carry forward, if your expenses exceeded the income earned at the new location in that year.

Students

Tuition paid to a post-secondary institution creates a credit, either for use by the student or by a spouse, supporting parent or grandparent. However, there is no advantage to paying the second term tuition in December, as it is only claimable in the period to which it applies.

If you have an RESP set up for your kids or grandkids, make a contribution by December 31 to collect a government grant of 20% on the first $2,500 of contribution. For children who turned 15 in the current year, December 31 is the last chance to set up a plan and get a grant for this year, and get eligibility for coming years.

For RESP withdrawals, choose carefully between calendar years, based primarily on the taxable income of the beneficiary student. For example, if the child will graduate and start earning full-time income next April, it likely makes more sense to withdraw taxable growth and grant in the current year.

RRSP contributions

Remember that if you turned 71 in the current year, you need to convert your RRSPs to RRIFs and LIRAs to LIFs prior to year end. You might also have a December 31 contribution deadline, IF you have contribution room.

Normally, the RRSP contribution deadline is 60 days after year end, usually March 1. However, if you turn 71 this year, your RRSP contribution deadline is December 31, not 60 days later, unless you are contributing to a spousal RRSP for a spouse who is under 71. (In that case, you have until March next year.) Check your CRA Notice of Assessment or call CRA directly to see if you have any contribution room. (A person will only have contribution room if they have undeducted contributions carried forward, or if they had "earned income" in the previous year.)

If you are 71 and you have earned income this year, you can also make contributions of 18% of that earned income for next year, the year in which you turn 72. If you make this contribution in December, you will pay a 1% penalty for the month of December, as you are actually making an over-contribution until January 1.

You will have the contribution room next year, but you don't have it yet, as it is based on the previous years' earned income. But again, if you have a younger spouse, you can continue to make spousal contributions, and won't need to have made yours in December, so no penalty.

Tax refunds and withholding at source

If you get a tax refund each year (thanks to deductions like RRSP or interest on an investment loan), consider using a T1213 form to request relief from deductions at source for next year, so you get the money into your hands every month during this year.

Similarly, if you have had your Old Age Security (OAS) clawed back but won't next year, use form T1213 (OAS) to ask for your OAS payments throughout the year, instead of waiting until CRA has assessed next year's tax return.

Medical expenses

Income tax filing deadline is April 30 (or June 15 for people who have self-employment income).

Here are a few tips relating to medical expenses. Remember that you do not have to use December 31 as your year end for medical expenses.

You can claim medical expenses for any 12 month period ending in the taxation year (as long as you have not previously claimed the expenses, of course). This could work to your advantage if you had, say, large expenses in November of one year and then February of the following year.

This is important as there is a deduction, of sorts—a threshold of the lesser of $2,011 or 3% of your net income, that you must overcome before your medical expenses earn a credit. You can combine expenses of two spouses and use the lower income to calculate the threshold, but make sure the spouse making the claim is paying tax, as this is another non-refundable credit.

Dependent family member's expenses may also be claimed, subject to another set of rules.

Eligible medical expenses include any out-of-pockets costs paid to a medical practitioner, most medical supplies and equipment (such as walkers, wheelchairs, hearing aids, crutches), required home renovations, and virtually any para-medical treatment that ends in "y." Travel and accommodation required to get care not available in your area may also be eligible, under certain conditions.

42

RRSPs and TFSAs—
Which is the Better Ride?

IS THE RRSP still the best way for you to fund your retirement, based on a criterion of what provides you with **the most net income in retirement**?

Or should you be maximizing your $5,000 per year contribution into a TFSA first, and only then using your additional cash to contribute to your RRSP?

For many people, the TFSA may be a superior long term plan.

The immediate tax relief from an RRSP contribution means that you can invest up to 40% more today (assuming you also invest your tax saving), and therefore you will have more money in a future RRSP than you would in a TFSA.

However, the tax you pay on the RRSP or RRIF withdrawal at retirement may kill that advantage, and more.

Here's an example of someone having $5,000 of savings capacity each year, so we can compare apples to apples. If you have more than $5000 per year to invest, then the RRSP will certainly be the approach for that extra savings capacity.

We will use a 35% marginal tax rate (MTR) today ($40,000 to $67,000 taxable income), and a 28% MTR in retirement (under $40,000). We assume that you contribute up to your annual RRSP contribution limit.

If your tax rate is higher now than our example, and will be as low or lower in retirement, then the RRSP is more favoured than in this example. On the other hand, if your rate is lower now, then you are likely best to choose the TFSA, and then additional non-registered equity investing for your surplus savings capacity.

Let's look at the example:

A $5,000 RRSP contribution reduces taxable income by $5,000. With a 35% MTR, this saves $1,750 in immediate taxes. If you add these two amounts together, then $6,750 can go into the RRSP this year, compared to $5,000 into the TFSA. Make sense?

If you can get $6,750 into an RRSP, you can actually get an additional tax saving on the refund as well, and therefore invest a total of $7,692 into the RRSP. (You can actually continue to increase your tax saving by contributing each additional tax reduction, but we'll stop here for now.)

The two ways to do this—if you don't have the additional cash—is either to borrow it, then pay back the loan as soon as you have the tax refund, or to contribute monthly throughout the year. The ideal is to adjust your paycheque withholdings at work, so you get the refund throughout the year, and can therefore invest more each month.

The process for adjusting your tax withholdings on your paycheques (as we discussed in our chapters on cash flow management) is to provide your employer with a completed Form T1213, Request to Reduce Tax Deductions at Source, which can be found on CRA's website or obtained from a tax office.

Our comparison is contributing $5,000 per year to a TFSA. In this case, there is no immediate tax saving, so the total you can invest is $5,000.

If you continue this contribution pattern for 30 years and earn 7% per year on average, then the TFSA will grow to about $472,000 and the RRSP will grow to about $638,000. (To get these returns, you must invest in good quality equities— you can't leave either account to languish in a savings account or a GIC.)

As predicted, the RRSP is larger, because you invested more money each year, partly funded by our good friends at the Canada Revenue Agency.

But let's look at after-tax retirement income.

A fairly safe retirement withdrawal rate is 5% of your portfolio, to reduce the likelihood of running out of money during your lifetime. (However, remember that CRA will force you to withdraw about 7.4% from your RRIF at age 71, whether you need it or not, and pay tax on that amount.)

At 5%, the RRSP pays out $31,900 before tax, while the TFSA will only pay out $23,600, but tax free. Which is better?

After deducting tax of 28%, or $8,932, on the RRSP or RRIF withdrawal, you would only have $22,968 to spend, slightly less than from the TFSA.

In fairness to the RRSP, after age 65 the first $2,000 of regular RRIF withdrawals are eligible for the Pension Credit, and you may be able to partly transfer the credit to or from your spouse, if there is a tax advantage to that. However, it is likely you could use that credit with other eligible pension income.

The relative advantage of the TFSA may increase when you look at income-tested government programs and tax credits that are only eligible at lower incomes. The RRIF income adds to net income for these tests, while the TFSA withdrawals do not. Also causing potential penalty for income-tested programs and credits are interest income, capital gains and dividends from non-registered investments.

For example, the Age Credit (65 and over) starts to be clawed back at $32,506 net of income, while the Medical Expense Credit can be more lucrative if Net Income is below $66,000. To the extent that extra income affects these amounts, it means an effective 25% extra "tax."

OAS is clawed back at a rate of 15% on net income above $67,000. At much lower incomes, where the OAS Supplement may be paid, there is a similar penalty for each dollar of additional income above the thresholds.

The advantage to committing to one plan or the other is that this will help force a savings discipline on you. Clearly, systematically saving into either an RRSP, TFSA—or even a non-registered investment account—will provide a more financially comfortable future than relying on an LRSP—the Lottery Retirement Savings Plan.

The most important thing is to commit to one or another if you want to get closer to financial independence.

NO BULL

Want financial independence? Commit to a regular TFSA or RRSP contribution plan.

Unfortunately, a lot of Canadians are doing neither, it appears.

A recent study by ING DIRECT[14] suggested that 87% of TFSA owners are only invested in savings vehicles and not using investment options—like stocks or equity mutual funds—with potential returns that can beat inflation and actually help fund retirement.

Most people appear to be only using their TFSA as an emergency fund, and 20% of the people in this study had already made withdrawals from a TFSA, and this was in the first four years of the program.

So, lesson number one in talking about any of these vehicles is to determine how much you need to save each month to fund your own retirement and other financial goals, and let your personal facts and needs help you determine which mix of vehicles to use.

---

[14] ING Direct, January 5, 2011; Angus Reid Public Opinion survey of 1,009 randomly selected Canadians. http://www.ingdirect.ca/en/aboutus/whoweare/whatwereupto/PR_2011-01-05.html

If you have enough money to fully fund both an RRSP and a TFSA, and you are in a high tax bracket, then generally you will want to maximize both. However, most people saving for retirement do not have unlimited funds, and must make choices.

If you have to choose between, and you are in a high tax bracket and want the immediate tax benefits, then the RRSP is likely the choice.

I recommend that you diligently track your own contributions and withdrawals because I have seen many CRA Notices of Assessment that told taxpayers they had unused TFSA contribution room, when in fact they had fully contributed. It appears that the system for reporting to taxpayers is way too slow, and therefore inaccurate. CRA is not yet aware of the recent contributions when they report to taxpayers, so they give them incorrectly high amounts of available room which, if followed, could result in penalties.

Again, as a reminder of the basics, there is no tax benefit for making a TFSA contribution, unlike an RRSP. The tax advantage comes when you earn investment income on your contribution. This could be in the form of interest, dividends or capital gains.

If you contribute $5,000 and earn 6% on it for five years, my 1982 Hewlett Packard 12C calculator tells me you will have almost $7,000 accumulated in your TFSA. There has been no tax on the investment income earned, and you can withdraw that $7,000 without any tax to pay.

That's the short term use of it as a savings or emergency funding vehicle.

In the long run, the TFSA can be a very effective tool for accumulating retirement income. If you contribute $5,000 per year for 30 years and average a 6% compounded return, the future value will be close to $425,000. Since your contributions will total $150,000, you will have earned some $275,000 of investment income tax-free.

While you can accumulate even more by making RRSP contributions and reinvesting the immediate tax saving resulting from your contribution deduction each year, your future RRSP withdrawals are fully taxable.

It's worthwhile to do some calculations, either on your own or with your advisor, to determine which mix of these approaches will be expected to provide you with the most after-tax retirement income.

If you are already retired, chances are you have non-registered investments or cash reserves earning investment income on which you are paying tax. The TFSA is a good place to shelter that, so maximize your benefit by fully contributing.

43

Keeping More of Your Investment Returns

I'VE HEARD PEOPLE ARGUE that there should be no tax at all on investment income. They make the case that tax was paid on the money when we earned it as employment or self-employment income. When we save and invest money from what's left over, we shouldn't have to pay tax on it again, when trying to make it grow.

While it may be hard to disagree with that logic, I can tell you that you won't win such an argument with the Canada Revenue Agency. A better strategy is to know how to reduce or eliminate tax—legally and within the rules—on your investment income.

You already know that all forms of investment income earned within an RRSP, RRIF, LIRA, LIF or TFSA is not taxable. Only the money withdrawn from the first group of accounts is taxable, and withdrawals from a TFSA are never taxable.

So, earning all of your investment income inside registered plans is one way to eliminate the tax on the investment income. That's all that many people ever need to know.

However, my wish for you is that you can maximize your RRSP and TFSA contributions each year, and continue to accumulate more investment capital outside these accounts, which will be exposed to taxation. Let's look at how that's treated.

Interest income is punished most severely. Perhaps this is because most investors take no risk to generate investment income. They put the money in savings accounts, GICs or savings bonds, typically, with a guaranteed return of capital, and often guaranteed investment returns.

Interest is taxed at your top marginal tax rate, on top of all other sources of income. Most people who are working full-time will pay tax of at least 25% on their interest, and often 35% or as much as 45%. Even when interest rates were high, this made it very difficult to beat inflation on an after-tax basis. At today's rates, it's impossible.

My advice is to try and earn all of your interest income on investments that are sheltered within your registered accounts, to avoid those punitive tax rates.

NO BULL

Try to shelter interest income inside registered plans, and earn dividends and capital gains outside.

If you own equity shares of companies, or mutual funds that invest in such stocks, then you will generally receive two different kinds of investment income. These are dividends and realized capital gains. (The type of investment income you want to avoid is realized capital losses.)

Dividends paid on large companies, usually publicly traded but also some privately held, are called "eligible" dividends. That means that the dividend you receive is eligible for a more generous dividend tax credit than "other than eligible" dividends, which are dividends paid by small private companies eligible for the special low tax rate on the first $400,000-$500,000 of profit (depending on the province).

The higher tax credit on eligible dividends acknowledges the fact that these large corporations have paid corporate tax at a much higher rate. The tax system attempts to equalize the net amount available to shareholders after the total of corporate and personal taxes is calculated.

When you sell corporate shares or mutual fund units (or any other capital property) at a profit, only half of the profit must be included in your income. The other half is tax-free.

The magic with capital gains is when you buy and hold a share or fund unit for many years, during which time it rises and falls in value, but ultimately doubles or triples. By holding onto it and not selling, you avoid "realizing" or crystallizing the capital gain, and you continue to defer the tax.

What does all this mean to you?

Ontario Marginal Tax Rates for 2012[15]

Taxable Income Range	Ordinary Income	Capital Gains	In-Eligible Dividends	Eligible Dividends
Up to $10,822	0%	0%	0%	0%
$10,823 to $39,020	20.05%	10.03%	2.77%	-1.89%
$39,021 to $42,707	24.15%	12.08%	7.90%	3.77%
$42,708 to $68,719	31.15%	15.58%	16.65%	13.43%
$68,720 to $78,043	32.98%	16.49%	17.81%	14.19%
$78,044 to $80,963	35.39%	17.70%	20.82%	17.52%
$80,964 to $85,414	39.41%	19.70%	23.82%	19.88%
$85,415 to $132,406	43.41%	21.70%	28.82%	25.40%
$132,407 to $500,000	46.41%	23.20%	32.57%	29.54%
Over $500,000	47.97%	23.98%	34.52%	31.69%

Source: *EverGreen Explanatory Notes*—Knowledge Bureau (www.knowledgebureau.com)

Notice that in the lowest tax bracket (lowest two in some provinces), the actual tax rate on dividend income is **negative.** This means that you will actually receive a net tax credit for earning dividend income. If you can take advantage of this phenomenon, then certainly do it.

Mutual fund investor—know thy tax treatment

If you are an investor in mutual funds outside of an RRSP, RRIF or TFSA, it pays to understand the tax treatment of mutual funds, and the difference between a mutual fund trust and a mutual fund corporation. And, since I like impossible missions, I will try to explain it all in understandable terms in 748 words.

Most mutual funds are structured as trusts. We'll get to corporations a little later. In this context, the trust is essentially a "transparent" entity. The mutual fund company acts as trustee, holding your money in trust for you. They have no beneficial ownership—the beneficial (actual) owners are you and the other unitholders. If the trustee were to go bankrupt, its creditors could not claim your money. For tax purposes, the transparency means that this trust acts as a "flow-through" entity, and any investment income generated by the fund's investments is flowed through proportionately to the unitholder investors.

---

[15] Updates are posted regularly in EverGreen Explanatory Notes and Knowledge Bureau Report, found at www.knowledgebureau.com. (Also see Evelyn Jacks, *Essential Tax Facts,* Winnipeg: Knowledge Bureau, 2012.)

For example, let's say the mutual fund invests mostly in Canadian stocks, ch pay dividends. The fund also holds cash reserves, which generate interest. fund also has expenses, the largest of which is the management fee charged he manager, plus legal, accounting, mailing costs and GST.

The interest and dividend income, reduced by the expenses, is allocated for purposes to the unit holders each year. These distributions are also available ash, but most unit holders choose wisely to have the distributions automati- 'y reinvested in more units. Some funds have a mandate to distribute earnings nthly or quarterly, as opposed to annually.

Whether you see the cash or not, you will receive a T3 reporting slip at the end the year for your share of the net taxable income. Often, the interest portion is offset by the expenses, and you end up with Canadian dividend income only. The dividends are treated in the same way they would be if you owned the underlying stocks directly. The dividend is grossed up, and then partly offset by a credit. All of this is calculated and shown on your T3 slip.

International mutual funds might also allocate to you things like foreign business income, foreign tax withheld, and foreign investment income. The foreign tax provides a credit which reduces your Canadian tax.

The second major form of income allocated to you from the fund will be realized capital gains. It makes sense that if the fund sold stocks at a profit during the year, and the total of the profitable sales exceeded sales that generated losses, a net capital gain will result. Your share of the net gain will show up on your T3 slip, but only half of the gain is taxable.

It might not make sense to you that you receive a taxable capital gain in a year when the stock market has declined and your fund has gone down in value, but this can happen. You might still receive an allocation of capital gains, if the fund had sold stocks at a profit. The lower value results from a general decline in price of the stocks still owned by the fund.

Remember, a capital gain is only realized when stocks are sold. If you own a fund that holds its stocks for many years while they appreciate, you could be deferring tax on your capital gain for many years, in the same way as if you've purchased a stock directly and held it for many years. The capital gain is only reported when the investment is sold and your total gains for that year exceed your total losses.

Note that if you use a "portfolio fund" (sometimes called "fund of funds"), which automatically re-balances among a number of underlying mutual funds, capital gains may be generated on the switches.

This brings us to mutual fund corporations. Many mutual funds are available in either a trust or corporate class version. The advantage to the corporate class is that a family of mutual funds with different mandates—like Canadian, international, small cap, bond or T-bill—are represented by different classes of shares in one corporation. This allows an investor to switch from one fund mandate to another without incurring capital gains.

In a mutual fund corporation, you are a shareholder, rather than a unit holder. With a long investment horizon, this corporate class approach can be valuable. Looking into the future, your objectives may change from primarily growth to primarily income. Being able to make that move without incurring tax on the capital gains you've deferred for many years could be a distinct advantage.

Remember, it's not just what you make—it's what you keep.

44

A Business as a
Tax Deduction

SALARIED EMPLOYEES sometimes envy business owners for their ability to deduct certain expenses, like entertainment of customers, travel to conferences and automobile expenses. (Less enviable are things like 18-hour days, financial stress and human resource issues, but we will leave that for another discussion.)

If certain conditions are met, salaried employees can enjoy the same benefits. They can start a business and deduct legitimate business expenses, even if those deductions result in a net loss for the business. As long as the business is set up as a proprietorship rather than a corporation, then the employee may be able to deduct those business losses on the personal tax return.

However, claiming business expenses can also put you in a higher risk category for an audit by CRA, and those expenses claimed will be rejected unless a number of conditions are met. This is true whether or not the business is incorporated.

It is normal for new businesses to lose money. The number of years before a profit is shown often depends on the type of business. It can be argued that a lawn care and snow clearing service, for example, should show a profit by the end of the second year, but a software company that needs two years to develop its product, then a year or two to bring customers on line, may require four or five years to establish itself and have income exceed expenses.

The losses may be deductible to the business proprietor during that period, and offset other income earned by that person. **However, in order to deduct an expense, you have to spend the money**, so don't look at this as a free ride. As well, the money must be a legitimate business expense, spent with the expectation of earning profit.

This section outlines the rules on deductibility and how to apply them. This knowledge will be very valuable if you decide to start a business. Keep in mind, though, that the reason to start a business is to make money. Ideally, this should be more than you are making by being an employee, and the business model provides the opportunity to grow in scale, add employees and become very profitable.

Alternatively, the business must be able to provide the entrepreneur with a good income and the independence that true entrepreneurs seek. If you contemplate starting a business, do it for the right reasons, and know that it can be risky, and the losses could set back your plans.

For expenses to be deductible, there has to be an actual business—a bona fide commercial activity. In tax terms, a "business" is an entity that actively tries to generate profit by providing goods and services.

Generally, any expenses incurred for the purpose of earning income are deductible from the profit of the business. However, the expenses must be paid out for the purposes of earning income, in order to be deductible. Currently, there is no legislative test which requires that there be a "Reasonable Expectation of Profit" ("REOP"), provided that the business and/or expense incurred in connection with the business are for "business" and not "personal" purposes.

Individuals can operate a business as a sole proprietorship, which means that the business and the person are essentially one and the same. This is the situation that gives rise to the personal deductions we are talking about here.

With a proprietorship (or partnership, if more than one proprietor), the gross income and net income of the business are shown on the tax return of the person who is the proprietor. If the business shows a loss, then that loss may be deductible against the person's other income. For example, if Bob has a salary of $60,000 and starts a business which loses $10,000 in its first year by deducting legitimate business expenses, then Bob can reduce his taxable income by $10,000 and pay less tax.

Consider staying unincorporated for the first year or two of starting a new business, if the expectation is a net loss initially (and there are no other good reasons to immediately incorporate, like limited liability).

If Bob's business had been incorporated from the start, then it is the corporation that would have the loss, and only the corporation would be able to carry it forward to deduct against future profits of the corporation. Bob would not have had a personal deduction for the business loss, because the loss belongs to the Corporation, and not to the shareholders.

An incorporated business

A corporation is a separate entity—a distinct "person"—from the shareholders, who are the owners. The property of the corporation belongs to the corporation, and not to the shareholders. Owners of incorporated businesses need to keep this point in mind when taking money from their business.

Every withdrawal of cash from the corporation payable to the owners needs to be classified as either salary, dividend or loan to a shareholder. There are very specific rules about paying back any loan from your own corporation.

Failure to stay within all of these rules can result in double tax under Section 15 of the Income Tax Act. Under these provisions, a shareholder draw can become taxable to the shareholder, and not deductible to the corporation. That's the worst situation to be in.

Any draw that is going to be considered salary (and this includes year-end bonuses) must have income tax withheld from it and sent to CRA, before the 15th of the month following. (More frequent remittance deadlines apply for larger employers who are "accelerated remitters.") The penalties are onerous for being even one day late, so take this obligation seriously.

Problems are created for business owners when corporate cheques are written to the owners without proper classification and proper tax withholding. Big problems can arise at year end, after which it may take several months for the business owner and accountant to calculate the net profit of the corporation and decide how much deductible bonus (classified as salary) should be paid to the owner/manager, in order to reduce the taxable income of the corporation and have it pay less tax.

The problem is that this payment is then classified—after the fact—as having been due to the shareholder at year end, so tax withholdings that had been required within the specified number of days after year-end are now automatically late.

Watch out for that, and avoid this by estimating the amount and sending the tax withholdings within the required deadlines.

Salaries and dividends are both taxable, but at different rates. To pay a dividend, the corporation must pay tax on the money first, so the tax rate applied to the shareholder recipient is lower than for salaries.

Salaries require payment of CPP premiums, and in some cases, EI premiums. Salaries create RRSP contribution room, while dividends do not.

Where a business is very profitable, most accountants still recommend paying enough salary to maximize CPP benefits. Some—but not all—accountants recommend paying enough salary to generate the maximum RRSP contribution. This is a holdover from the days when the small business tax rate was about 23% and the combination of corporate tax and personal tax on the dividend was higher than salary alone. That's no longer the case, as most provinces have dramatically decreased the tax rate on the first $400,000 to $500,000 of small business profit, to as low as 12%.

Paying a dividend to a shareholder spouse or child over 18 who has very little other income can result in a significant net tax saving for the family. As well, any corporate profit not needed by the shareholders can be left behind in the corporation to be invested there.

This can result in a significant long-term tax deferral, with the corporation investing 88 cents of each dollar, after-tax. This means much more money can be invested, compared to paying personal tax at rates as much as 46%, or tax on personal dividends at over 37%.

There is a lot of planning that goes into running a business, in addition to making sure that the business is successful. We have just scraped the surface here. To do more reading on this, we recommend:

1. *Building a Dream—A Canadian Guide to Starting Your Own Business* by Walter S. Good; and
2. *Master Your Investment in the Family Business* by Larry Frostiak and Jenifer Bartman.

My overriding rule when deciding on a tax filing position is to absolutely disclose every source of income. Income is black and white, and failure to disclose income is a violation of the Income Tax Act.

On the other hand, you can take a more aggressive filing stance with deductions, as long as you sincerely believe that they fit within the rules and that you actually made the expenditure for the purpose of earning income. If you lose the argument, you will likely pay interest (at CRA's high rates) on the unpaid taxes, but only because you got use of the money during that period of time.

Keep in mind that many people have tried to deduct illegitimate business expenses over the years, only to have them rejected after a CRA review or audit, and then having to pay interest and, in some cases, penalties. It's best to only claim deductions that you believe will stand up to an audit.

45

Divide and Conquer

WE TOUCHED ONLY BRIEFLY on the third "D" of tax planning—**Divide**.

With your knowledge of Canada's progressive tax system, you know the goal is to minimize the amount of tax that any one individual claims in the higher tax brackets, and the fact that every person pays more tax on their last dollar of income than on their first.

For example, two individuals each with taxable income of $50,000 will pay total tax of $19,040. However, one person with taxable income of $100,000 will pay $28,000, about $9,000 more than the two people.

There are a number of political and sociological reasons for this result, some of which you may agree with and some you will disagree with, but you can't argue with the mechanics and the result. Higher income earners pay a higher rate of tax, and the more income taxed in the higher brackets, the higher the overall tax rate for that individual.

As we saw above, dividing the income in half provides a huge tax benefit. So, naturally CRA has rules against this, commonly called the attribution rules. Let's look at an example.

If, in our example of $100,000 income, we had $60,000 of employment income and $40,000 of investment income, we would be tempted to suggest that the individual's spouse claim the investment income. That would save the couple a significant amount of tax.

Not so fast. The rules say that whoever earned the investment capital on which the subsequent investment income is earned must claim that subsequent investment income on his or her tax return. The same is true for other types of income—he or she who earns it must claim it.

Setting up a corporation and having different family members as the share-holders so the dividends can be split can help between spouses, as long as each spouse has contributed equal amounts of capital toward setting up the corporation, or the business that will split its profits. However, there are significant restrictions here on dividends paid to children under 18. Popularly called the "kiddie tax," this rule imposes the top tax rate on any dividends paid to minor children through corporations controlled by their parents.

So what solutions are available to us, to divide income and reduce taxes?

- **Spousal RRSP contributions.** The spousal system allows the higher income spouse to claim the deduction on the RRSP contribution, but contribute it into the account of the spouse who will have the expected lower income in retirement, when the RRSP is expected to be withdrawn.

- **Pension transfer.** As of 2008, people who receive qualifying pension income can transfer up to 50% of that pension income onto a spouse's tax return.

- **Accumulate investment income in the name of the lower income spouse.** Legitimately, up to 100% of the lower income spouse's gross income can be invested into a non-registered investment (over and above RRSP and TFSA) and the lower income spouse claims the investment income.

- **Loans to a spouse at the CRA prescribed rate.** If the higher income spouse has more investment capital then can be transferred or shared using the methods above, we can get radical, and take advantage of the historically low rate that CRA requires to be charged on loans between spouses. The current rate is 1%. This means that if Robert, who is in the top tax bracket and has $300,000 of non-registered capital to invest loans that money to his wife Greta, she can invest it and claim all of the investment income, as long as she actually pays him $3000 per year in interest, paid within 30 days of each year end. She can deduct this interest but he must claim it on his taxes.

- **Gifts of investment capital to a spouse.** If Robert instead gifted the $300,000 to Greta, he would have to claim all of the investment income earned on the initial $300,000 and on any reinvested income. However, if Greta withdrew any investment capital earned, she could invest that money and legitimately claim it on her tax return. This is a slower method, but also works.

- **Gifts or loans to minor children.** These are more complicated, since minors cannot enter into a legal contract, but we will leave that to you and your lawyer. The tax rules are slightly different for children and spouses, and this creates some opportunities. If Robert gave the $300,000 to little Bobby to invest, Robert would have to claim any interest or dividends earned on the investment capital, but little Bobby would be able to claim any realized capital gains on his return. Therefore, the strategy is to invest strictly for capital gains and not for regular investment income. The real complication is that the money must really be gifted, and little Bobby does not have to give it back.

The attribution rules are complicated, and this is not an area to enter into without good professional advice. However, the potential reduction in taxes can be significant for someone who has accumulated significant amounts of investment capital.

For all of us, the necessary goal is to try and arrange equal incomes for retirement, to keep the family tax bill as low as possible when we are living on our capital.

46

Educating Rita
(and Britney
and little Robbie)

THERE ARE FOUR BASIC WAYS to pay for your child's (or grandchild's) post-secondary education.

Another option, which I endorse, is to make it clear to them from day one that they will be paying for it themselves.

OK, never mind. Here are the other four:

1. Pay at the time the money is needed, out of after-tax dollars. This is **not** the most efficient, and will only work if you plan to be making a lot of money when they start school, or be willing to sacrifice other things at that time.

2. Contribute to a Registered Education Savings Plan (RESP) starting as early as possible, which provides a government grant equal to 20% of any annual contribution up to $2,500, plus tax sheltering on the investment income earned in the plan. It is also a way to set aside money that is clearly earmarked for education. More on the pros and cons later.

3. Put money away systematically into a non-registered investment account, or a formal "in-trust" account, targeted for education. If it is the parent's or grand-parent's money, then interest and dividends earned on this account must be declared each year on the tax return of the contributor. However, capital gains are claimable by the child. (On the other hand, any investment capital that comes from what the child earns, inherits or receives as "reasonable" gifts on special occasions, creates investment income that is taxable to the child.)

    "In-trust" accounts are actually fraught with complications. Before setting one up, speak at length with both an advisor and a lawyer who are familiar with the pitfalls, and can create a trust agreement for you.

4. Buy a permanent (whole life or universal life) insurance policy on the life of the child. This can work as a partial funding method only. Such a policy has many other side advantages, but I don't recommend it as the primary education savings tool. However, it can provide life insurance at a low rate, substantial cash value in the policy by age 18, and guarantee the child's future insurability. These are all valuable benefits, but they are generally lost if you cash in the policy for education.

Registered Education Savings Plans

For pure education funding, I give the nod to the RESP for most families. The 20% Canadian Education Savings Grant (CESG) on the first $2,500 per child per year means an extra $500 each year to invest. If it compounds at 8% each year, the grant alone will be worth over $18,000 when the child is 18.

The tax sheltering on the growth also helps. The growth will be taxable to the child as the money is withdrawn while attending university or other post-secondary education, but the child will generally be in a low tax bracket at that time, often paying no tax at all. The child also gets to use the tuition, education and textbook credits.

The original capital that you contribute can be withdrawn tax-free at any time.

For many people, the biggest single advantage is the discipline and commitment such a plan provides. If you can afford $208.33 per month, you can have over $110,000 put aside for education by the time the child is ready to start school, if it averages 8% and you start in their first year. (If you get a 10% return, the value will exceed $135,000.) That money will continue to earn investment income until spent and should provide a very good start on anything but an Ivy League university.

If you have more than one child, we suggest a family plan RESP, which allows you to allocate the contributions and withdrawals to the different beneficiaries, as needed. The reality is that not all children will attend post-secondary institutions, and a family plan allows for some flexibility.

Worst case, if no beneficiary attends any type of post secondary education—which can be community college, art or technical schools, as well as universities—then the government grant has to be paid back, but not the earnings thereon. The growth component must either be transferred to the contributor's RRSP (if contribution room exists) or withdrawn and be taxed.

Even in this case, however, the original contributed capital can be withdrawn tax free, since there was no tax deduction provided for the deposit originally.

When it comes to taking out the money, the student will need to contact the educational institute to provide "Proof of Enrollment." This is a more formal and specific document than the tuition receipt, and must be requested specifically each year.

The resulting withdrawal, called an Education Assistance Payment (EAP) is capped at $5,000 for the first withdrawal. Note that the money can be used for virtually anything related to education, including tuition, room and board, textbooks, laptops. No receipts need be shown to anyone.

If you need more detail on any of these items, go to www.hrsdc.gc.ca/eng/learning/education_savings/index.shtml

Now, hit the books, kids!

47

Disability Tax Credit is Badly Under Claimed

THE DISABILITY TAX CREDIT ("DTC") is significant, as it reduces tax by about $1,500 per year for a person who qualifies, or for the supporting person of a dependent who qualifies. I have found there are a surprising number of people with a physical or mental impairment of some kind, or a family member living with a disability.

A person does not have to be disabled to claim this credit. People who have a significant health problem which causes that person to be "significantly restricted in activities of basic living" may qualify. The DTC is also the qualification measure for a host of other tax programs for people with disabilities, which makes proper assessment especially critical.

As well, once approved, you may be able to file adjustments to your previous income tax returns dating back to the onset of your impairment, for up to 10 years.

Taxpayers who have "a severe and prolonged impairment in mental or physical functions" may qualify for the DTC, even though they might still be able to work. This is quite different from the definition of disability under a disability insurance policy or disability benefits under the Canada Pension Plan.

Many people who would qualify for the DTC are not claiming it, and I believe that the number of legitimate claims are not accepted, because the application form is very complex and often incorrectly or incompletely filled out by the medical professional or other "Qualified Practitioner." As a result, there is actually a thriving business for consultants who can help people through this maze, in return for a fee that may be as much as one third of the credit recovered.

CRA specialists have told me that, since the DTC Certification form itself weeds out most applicants who would not qualify, most applications are accepted, provided they are properly completed.

For the medical certification, CRA depends on the qualified practitioner who has completed the Disability Tax Credit Certificate, Form T2201. Since it is a complicated form (at least to me) and medical practitioners tend to be very busy, this part of the process may be the real challenge.

Start with CRA's website www.CRA.GC.ca/disability and click on "Are you eligible?" By answering the questions asked, you are led through the process. CRA has improved this significantly since 2009, with examples and illustrations.

I have helped clients successfully with this process, but have several times had to go back to the doctor for a correction to the certification form before submitting it. I find the logic of the form complex to follow, unfortunately. That may be one reason why some people who might qualify have not applied.

Definitions

Here are shortened definitions taken from CRA pamphlet RC 4064 and found online at http://www.cra-arc.gc.ca/E/pub/tg/rc4064/README.html. If you think that you or a family member may qualify, carefully read through all this information before proceeding, or call 1-800-959-8281.

- **Markedly restricted**—you are markedly restricted if all, or substantially all of the time, you are unable (or it takes you an inordinate amount of time) to perform one or more of the basic activities of daily living.
- **Significantly restricted**—means that although you do not **quite** meet the criteria for markedly restricted, your ability to perform a basic activity of daily living is still substantially restricted.
- **Basic activities**—speaking, hearing, walking, feeding, dressing, mental functions necessary for everyday life, bowel or bladder functions.
- **Prolonged**—has lasted, or is expected to last, for a continuous period of at least 12 months.
- **Qualified practitioner**—medical doctors, optometrists, audiologists, occupational therapists, physiotherapists, psychologists and speech-language pathologists.

According to the self-assessment questionnaire, anyone who has a prolonged impairment that *markedly* restricts them in one of the activities, or *significantly* restricts two or more of the activities, or the person is blind or receiving life-sustaining therapies, will likely qualify.

Many of these terms are subjective, and "daily activities" need not mean "every single day." If the criterion was "unable" to perform activities, that would be straightforward. However, "taking an inordinate amount of time" is subjective and largely up to the medical practitioner to observe and certify.

If a person qualifies for the DTC and has employment or self-employment income, that person may also qualify for Line 453—the working income tax benefit disability supplement, which is a separate application described in CRA pamphlet RC4227.

A child under 18 who is eligible for the disability amount may also be eligible for the Child Disability Benefit. See pamphlet T4114 or visit the Benefits section on the CRA website. There are a number of other government programs for people with disabilities or people who need attendant care, or their family members who are caregivers.

A little research could go a long way.

When I completed my late father's DTC application after he passed away, I discovered that the credit can also be applied posthumously. In his case, the disability had actually been in place for three years, so the credit was received for those three tax years.

Registered Disability Savings Plan (RDSP)

Qualifying for the DTC also allows a person to open an RDSP. Depending on family income, this could mean annual government grants of up to $3,500.

The RDSP is roughly based on the RESP model, and also shelters investment growth from tax until the money is withdrawn, when it is taxed to the beneficiary.

You can look on the CRA website, or go to www.rdsp.com, or my blog www.davidchristianson.com, for more information.

Managing the Bull:
Detect and Deflect the Crap

REDUCING YOUR INCOME TAX BURDEN and reinvesting the money toward your financial independence can go a long way toward helping you get there. Planning now to pay less income tax in your retirement will mean enjoying a better lifestyle down the road, with less pressure on your investments and other resources.

We've shown you a number of ways to avoid paying more than your fair share of income taxes, and talked about some significant tax saving strategies.

- Strive to earn only dividends and deferred capital gains in your non-registered investment accounts, and shelter the interest income within RRSPs.
- Take full advantage of all available deductions and credits, by informing yourself about what's available.
- If your tax bracket warrants it, strive to maximize your RRSP contributions each year for the immediate tax reduction and the ongoing deferral of investment income, and then top off your TFSA accounts to take advantage of additional tax free growth.
- Split income with family members where possible, and where the rules allow.
- If appropriate for you, it may make sense to borrow to invest in income producing investments or real estate, and deduct the interest from your taxable income.
- You can use the RESP to collect government grants and shelter investment income and, in special circumstances, possibly collect the Disability Tax Credit and open an RDSP.

As you are successful in reducing your taxes, here's a suggestion—take a big portion of those tax savings and devote them to the achievement of your financial objectives. Whether those goals are to eliminate debt, buy a house, retire sooner or take a world tour, tax efficiency can help you reach them.

Whatever your key goals, use these extra resources toward them.

Developing some meaningful knowledge in the tax department and arranging your affairs to minimize your annual tax liability—both now and in retirement—can go a long way toward improving your lifestyle, without any sacrifices and without any risk.

Part 6

Protecting the Bull: Tackling Risk Management

You don't know what you got,
Until you lose it.

- GEORGE BURTON AND PAUL HAMPTON, 1961

48

Protecting the Ranch— Property and Casualty Insurance

THERE ARE ALL SORTS OF RISKS in everyday life. Protection can be purchased to guard against the negative financial effects of many of those risks.

This chapter focuses on protecting your property, and protecting you from the liability associated with someone being injured while on your property, or you causing injury to someone else.

A wise thing to do in thinking about insurance is to consciously think about how much of each risk you are able to assume yourself, and how much you want to transfer to an insurance company. Usually, this decision centres on whether or not you could financially bear the potential loss, rather than on how likely the loss is to occur.

For example, could you afford to replace your house if it burned down? If the answer is "absolutely not," and such a disaster would ruin you financially, then you really need to have comprehensive insurance on your house, even though the likelihood of your particular house burning down is extremely remote.

NO BULL

If you can't afford a loss, then buy insurance.

(Having said that a house burning down is a remote possibility, I have to point out that two people I know have seen their modern, expensive houses burn to the ground in the last three years, something I never expected to see.)

My advice here is to thoroughly review your coverage, ideally with an experienced insurance broker who specializes in the type of property you own and the risks to which you may be subject. Take the time with an expert to customize your coverage.

On May 19, 1994 we switched insurance brokers. You will understand in a minute why I recall the date so well. The new broker insisted on coming out to see the house and inspecting the property. Thank goodness she did, as she suggested to my wife that our old neighborhood with its mature trees was prone to sewage backup problems, with the possibility of tree roots getting into the lines and partly blocking them.

My wife asked, "How much?" and was told $14 extra. She hemmed and hawed a little, but thought that I would think it was a good idea, so she said yes. She wrote a post-dated cheque dated June 21, as requested, and the policy immediately went into effect.

The rain started the morning of Saturday, June 20 and did not stop until the storm drains were overwhelmed at nine o'clock Sunday night, at which time four feet of sewage backup had filled our basement before receding. The next day, the insurance company cashed our cheque.

Our old house had a finished basement, with a wooden ceiling built onto wooden walls, supported by a wood floor. All had to be torn out. As well, we stored lots of things in the basement, including my wife's collection of sewing patterns.

The insurance company replaced everything with a claim that approached $60,000. They were great, and accepted our documentation. They insisted on paying full replacement value for the patterns, even though they had been used and likely had no residual value.

The downside was that this disaster and several others prompted all casualty insurance companies to significantly limit the amount of coverage they offer for sewage backup or water damage.

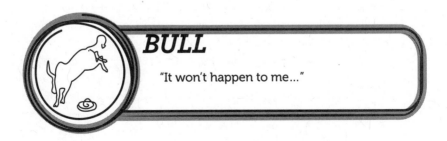

BULL

"It won't happen to me..."

For our part, we dug up the basement floor and installed a proper sump pit, sump pump and backup protection valve, to prevent a recurrence.

There are risks against which you can take precautions, some of which are quite simple. The obvious ones include not leaving paint-soaked rags around the garage, keeping your furnace and electrical wiring in good repair, locking your car and not leaving it running when you go into the convenience store. Make sure your eaves troughs are clear and your downspouts drain well away from your house. At the first sign of roof damage or shingles wearing out, carry out any necessary repairs.

On your house insurance, make sure your coverage is full replacement value on both the dwellings and the contents. Check right now on the total amount of your coverage, as it may be woefully inadequate if it hasn't been increased in the last five years.

With the rapid increase in house values and, especially, the incredible escalation in building costs lately, the replacement cost of the house is a lot more than it used to be. The old guideline of $100 per square foot has been replaced by $200 per square foot, or much more for a high-end house or anything in a remote location. That increase in construction costs makes a huge difference in rebuilding a house or cottage, or repairing damage.

The same could be true of your house or cabin contents. Make sure those special items like jewellery, furs and fine art are separately scheduled. Otherwise, the coverage will likely be limited to an amount much smaller than replacement value, with no coverage for water, humidity and other miscellaneous damage.

By "scheduling" any such valuables you can guarantee full replacement value and comprehensive coverage, often including "unexplained disappearance." Some insurance policies will also allow you to receive the cash equivalent, and not require you to replace the item. This type of flexible benefit coverage can even apply to your house or other buildings. Some companies do not require you to re-build.

To help with a claim, take photographs or make videos of the contents of your house, including items stored in the basement and garage. Store these pictures somewhere other than your house, like a safety deposit box, your office or a friend's house.

If you run a home-based business, think carefully about the potential dangers and losses that could occur if your house was burgled. Do you have customer lists or confidential customer financial information? What about your own company records and computer? A loss could have huge financial, business and privacy ramifications.

Make sure confidential papers are safely tucked away, preferably in a fireproof safe.

Make sure your liability coverage is adequate in the event that you make a mistake that causes damage (anywhere in the world), or someone has an accident on your property. You can be sued if someone trips on unrepaired concrete or step damage, or if they fall on ice or snow on your property. This applies whether you have invited the person onto your property or not.

We recently reviewed our home insurance policy. This includes not only the protection on our house for damage from fire or other disasters, but also the coverage on the contents and on personal liability risk, in the event that someone should be hurt on our property, or if we are found negligent for third party property or bodily injury damage worldwide.

Here are a few disturbing things we found out:

- Our insured value on the house was way too low. The huge increase in construction and material costs meant that we would only be able to rebuild a house half the size of ours.
- While we thought we had replacement value on the dwelling and outbuildings, that insufficient insured value meant actual replacement would be impossible.
- Our then-current sewer backup insurance, while in place, would only cover up to $4,000 of damages, in spite of a hefty premium. As mentioned earlier, this coverage is now limited or unavailable, and ours was clearly inadequate for a house with a finished basement, appliances and storage. The best protection is a working sump pump and backup valve, with a high water alarm added in. This is what we installed, and it has since saved the basement though several monsoons.
- While our personal property and contents limit seemed to be high enough overall, our coverage was severely restricted on individual items. This meant that our few valuable pieces of art and jewelry would not be covered for full value. We needed to schedule these valuable individual items, which meant individually appraising and valuing.
- Our liability coverage for personal injury and third party property damage might not be sufficient, in an age where Canadian claims are becoming more Americanized, which means much larger. We also wanted to add a large "umbrella liability" clause—we were thinking $5 million maximum—that would lay on top of our car and other insurance, for extra large liability claims.
- Our coverage did not insure damage by our pets. That was a shock, as we once had to replace a carpet after the dog had knocked over a can of paint. (Yes, we still have the dog...)

Clearly, we had to make some changes. These added to the cost of insurance, but we were able to counterbalance most of that increase by investigating the various discounts available for things like being claims free for five years, being within five kilometers of a fire hall and having a local fire hydrant, being mortgage free and having achieved a certain age threshold. As well, we increased our deductible, which decreased the premium significantly. This made our policy into more of a protection device against major disaster, but no longer covering small things like bike thefts.

Owners of luxury properties with high-value items among the contents, and owners of recreational vehicles or multiple properties would be wise to talk to an insurance specialist who focuses on such higher-end properties and the risks to which affluent people may be exposed.

NO BULL

Recreational properties and motorized toys expose the owners to significantly higher liability risk.

Since many of our clients are in this position, we work with firms that specialize in risk assessment and protection for affluent people. When we first started with them, they asked me questions about things I would never have thought about, in terms of insurance needs. For example, do I serve on the boards of any corporations or non-profit organizations? Do I know what liability insurance those groups have in place? Do we have any exotic trips planned? Do we employ domestic employees? (Yeah, right...) Do I have any corporations or trusts which own real estate or other physical property? Are my personal liability limits consistent across all major exposures?

Owners of expensive homes, especially, should focus on loss prevention through superior protection measures. Such preventative measures offer significant value in terms of both premium reduction and available maximum coverage, but most importantly, they help prevent loss and claims on the insurance. Protecting against those higher risks often means specialized coverage, and higher premiums, for more peace of mind.

49

Protecting Your Earning Power— Your Most Valuable Asset

YOU HAVE AN ASSET that's more valuable than your house—your ability to earn income. If your earning power were to be cut short due to death, the results could be devastating for your family. Term life insurance is a cheap way to protect against that danger until your investment assets become adequate and your responsibilities decrease. Your planning may also include permanent life insurance. More on this in the next chapter.

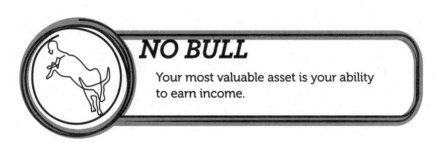

NO BULL

Your most valuable asset is your ability to earn income.

What if you get sick or injured and can't work? Disability insurance is the risk management tool. Make sure that you understand your coverage, the amount of your monthly benefit, maximum limits, the waiting period for your particular coverage and whether or not your benefits are taxable.

Critical illness (CI) insurance is a useful addition—*but not a replacement*—for disability insurance. CI policies pay a tax-free lump sum of money if you are hit with any one of 30 or so significant illnesses. You can use the money to take more time off from work, relieve financial stress, pay for treatment in another country and focus on getting better, or replace your retirement savings program.

Speaking of your health...

Your health is where you should take the most precautions. Obviously eating well, getting regular exercise, finding ways to decrease stress and avoiding damaging habits like smoking or excessive drinking are good ideas. Think long term—if you can almost guarantee that you will feel better and be able to do more 10 or 20 years from now, isn't it worth a little adjustment in your behaviour today?

We all know about preventing heart disease, but recent research has also shown that Alzheimer's may be delayed or prevented by eating a diet rich in green vegetables like spinach and broccoli, likely because the vegetables are rich in folic acid and antioxidants.

Keeping your cholesterol, weight and blood pressure down helps with these diseases and a range of others—and it may even save you money on your life insurance premiums. Many companies have a "preferred" rate for healthy people on their term policies. This saves you money and I can tell you, from personal experience, that there is nothing more satisfying than having an insurance company tell you they will bet their own money you are going to live longer than the average person.

Take charge of your own health—you'll be living inside that body for a long time.

50

Which Needs are Temporary and Which are Permanent?

AT ITS ESSENCE, life insurance is very straightforward—if you die, the insurance company pays the agreed amount.

Things can get more complicated when deciding on the amount of coverage you need and the right product, but we can simplify that by talking about **temporary needs** and **permanent needs**.

Remember that life insurance is simply the guaranteed delivery of dollars on death. If the death of a certain person would create a financial hardship for others, then insurance is often the best solution.

NO BULL

Life insurance is simply the guaranteed delivery of tax-free dollars on death.

These needs might be temporary—like paying off a mortgage or replacing a breadwinner's income while children are young—and therefore best addressed through term insurance. Or the needs might be permanent—like paying the estimated income taxes when the second one of a married couple dies—and best addressed by permanent insurance. This goes by names such as whole life, universal life, or term-to-100.

Term insurance is much less expensive initially, because the risk of a healthy person dying during the initial term is relatively low. Most people outlive their term insurance policies. These are generally not renewable after a certain age, like 70 or 75, and they become impossibly expensive as a policy owner gets older.

Permanent insurance costs more at the outset, partly because it usually builds up cash reserves, and also because the policy is required to pay out at some point in the future, as long as the policy owner keeps the policy in force. With most policies, the premium is set when issued, and will not increase in the future. This means the policy remains affordable through advanced age, and can stay in place until death.

Are your risks temporary or permanent?—
Term and whole life defined

The real question to ask is whether or not your insurance is properly matched to your actual needs, focusing on which needs will exist for a set period of time, and which will last your whole life.

Permanent insurance comes in.the form of whole life, term-to-100, or universal life. Term insurance can be yearly renewable term, or 5-year, 10-year, or 20-year renewable. Virtually every policy has a guaranteed renewal option at the end of those terms, but the premium will take a jump. Most are also convertible to permanent insurance, regardless of health.

When a term policy is initially issued, the insurance company signs a contract that guarantees the maximum premium payable on each renewal until the maximum age is reached, and guarantees it will continue to provide this insurance at those premium amounts, whether you are then healthy and insurable, or not.

When talking about term versus permanent insurance, another fact to lay on the table is that sales commissions are higher for permanent insurance, as both the percentage commission and the premium base on which the commission is calculated are higher. This may motivate your insurance agent toward permanent insurance.

This fact often leaves insurance agents and brokers vulnerable to criticism. Sometimes this criticism is justified. For example, when a family has a huge need for immediate insurance to cover one breadwinner while the children are young, the bulk of this need is temporary, and the actual need for death benefit protection is high, and may easily exceed $1 million. Protecting against that immediate risk is the need that should take priority over any consideration of retirement saving through life insurance, or enhancing estate value at the end of a normal life expectancy.

If an agent tries to sell the client a whole life policy with a much smaller death benefit, they do the client a disservice. If the family could only afford $100 per month for insurance premiums, for example, that might provide the right amount of term insurance, but only a small fraction of the necessary immediate protection if purchased through a whole life policy.

Occasionally, when people come to our office for their financial planning checkup, we find that they are paying high premiums for a small amount of insurance that is not adequate for their needs because they have a traditional whole life policy, rather than an appropriate amount of affordable term insurance. In this example, the type of insurance is not matched to the type of need, and therefore an adequate amount is seldom affordable.

Does this mean that term insurance is always the right solution, as some people would have you believe? My answer is no, term insurance is not always the right solution. Most financial writers and other pundits are not advisors, as I am. They don't counsel fifty-year-olds, sixty-year-olds and even seventy-year-olds who have a current need for life insurance. I see that quite often.

The cost is extremely high if you have to purchase life insurance at any of those ages, or if you have to convert a term policy to permanent at that time.

Purchasing permanent insurance early, in anticipation of a future insurance need, can result in much lower premiums over your lifetime. The flip side of that argument is that you pay the premiums for many more years, but in most policies you actually build equity. If you ultimately don't need the coverage in the future, you have a cash value that can be returned to you, or can be used to pay for a reduced amount of paid-up insurance. In this case, you can have permanent insurance in place until you die, with no further premiums payable.

Many insurance professionals would suggest that permanent insurance is "owning" insurance and paying for it over time, while term insurance is really "renting" coverage. That's good sales technique, but there is actually a lot of truth in it. Keep in mind that there are lots of examples in life where renting is more appropriate than purchasing. If you only need to use the asset (whether it's a car, cottage, water pump or paint sprayer) for a limited period of time, renting can be much more economical than an outright purchase.

It's only if you will be using the product (or insurance coverage) for a long enough period of time that purchasing can make more sense than renting.

NO BULL

Only permanent insurance guarantees protection against permanent needs, like taxes in the estate.

Examples of temporary needs:
- income replacement while there are outstanding debts
- young children in the home
- one spouse out of the work force
- waiting for retirement assets to accumulate to an adequate amount to ensure financial independence for both spouses.

Examples of permanent needs are:
- to pay income taxes on death (especially on the death of a second spouse, as the tax liability can be deferred until the second death)
- to cover last expenses like burial and professional fees
- to fund or increase charitable donations or bequests to family members on death, and
- any other need for guaranteed dollars on death, whenever that death might occur.

Since income taxes on capital gains and cashing in of RRSP or RRIF assets on death are only payable when the second spouse dies, insurance companies have developed specialized permanent policies to address this need. These are called joint last-to-die policies, which pay out the death benefit when the second spouse dies.

Since the likelihood of both spouses dying early is lower than one spouse dying early, the premiums on these are significantly reduced, compared to a policy on one personal loan. Therefore, joint and last-to-die policies make a lot of sense for the specific need of estate liquidity when taxes are due.

Most people have a blend of temporary and permanent needs. Match your coverage to your need, get good advice on the products, and you'll be fine.

51

Determining YOUR Insurance Needs

DURING THE WORKING YEARS, the engine of every family's financial machine is the ability to earn income from employment or self-employment. If the person earning that money dies, typically the income stops. Replacing this income is both the largest and most important need for life insurance for most families, unless they have accumulated enough assets that this income could be replaced through investment income, the sale of the business or other means.

That doesn't usually happen until later in one's working life.

This need for cash on death can vary widely. With a young family starting out with young children, with a mortgage and perhaps other debts, and one primary income earner, this need for insurance can be very large. Hopefully, it is a temporary need which will start to decrease significantly once the children are grown and independent, debts are paid off and other assets are accumulated, or if the other spouse starts to earn a similar income.

On the other hand, a childless working couple with equal incomes and no debts would have a much lower need for insurance, and might even decide (based on the

NO BULL

Not everyone needs life insurance. However, if you need it to protect your family, get it.

income needs of the surviving spouse), that they don't need any life insurance at all, provided they have enough liquid assets to cover off the immediate cash needs detailed in the forms below.

A person with no dependents—no one depending on the income that would stop on death—may have no need at all for life insurance, unless they have a desire to leave money to charitable groups or individuals. (We could argue that they don't even need insurance to pay off debts... as long as no one was depending on receiving value from the estate.)

Paying off debts is often the second most important factor in determining insurance needs. There are also other costs of dying that must be considered, including funeral costs, provincial probate fees, legal and professional fees, taxes (usually only if there is no surviving spouse), education funding, possibly child support or alimony obligations, personal and charitable bequests and other legacy wishes.

The exercise of determining life insurance needs is typically called a **capital needs analysis**.

There are more sophisticated ways to do it, but this form below will give you a general guideline. The first step in calculating need is to create a snapshot of the situation, assuming the spouse in question had died yesterday. Be realistic about the needs of the family, which will be very close to the total needs when both spouses are living. (Once complete, go through the same exercise for the other spouse, assuming the other one had passed away.)

Survivor income need

Family income needed (annual, before tax)	$_____
Minus:	
Survivor income (surviving spouse employment, pension rental income, etc.)	$_____
CPP survivor benefit	$_____
Investment income (if any)	$_____
Other income or support payments (rec'd)	$_____
Additional income need	$_____
Capital needed to provide that income	$_____ (1)

Assuming a 5% pretax return, the capital need is 20 times the amount of the income. This means replacing $50,000 of income requires $2 million of life insurance.

If you assume a lower rate of return, then the capital need increases. A more sophisticated way to calculate this includes an allowance for inflation, but could include a net present value calculation for any temporary needs, and assume the use of capital over the time period of the need.

Other capital needs at death

Final expenses (funeral, probate, legal, executor fees)	$_____
Income taxes (zero if leaving a surviving spouse)	$_____
Mortgage payout amount	$_____
All other debts	$_____
Education (present value of future needs)	$_____
One-time gifts, bequests or charitable contributions	$_____
Total other capital needs	**$_____ (2)**
Total capital needs (1+2)	**$_____ (3)**

Capital assets available to provide income (not included above)

Current life insurance amounts (death benefit) (employer group, professional association, personal)	$_____
Amount of any life insurance on existing loans	$_____
Other income-producing assets (investments, real estate, etc.) (not included above as producing investment income)	$_____
Total capital available on death	**$_____ (4)**
Additional life insurance need (3-4)	**$_____**

If insurance is needed to protect your family, don't scrimp. If the need is large, you may only be able to afford term insurance, but put that protection in place.

52

Protect Your Family, Not Your Mortgage Lender

WHEN YOU TAKE OUT a loan or a mortgage, you are offered the opportunity to life insure that mortgage with your financial institution. Should you sign up?

Whether you are borrowing from a bank, trust company, credit union or other lending institution, this coverage is almost certain to be offered. The institution makes money selling this insurance, and they also protect themselves from any possibility of default on the loan as a result of the borrower dying. The incentives to bank employees to sell such profitable extras can even prompt some to suggest that this is mandatory.

The institutions generally offer disability insurance coverage on the loans as well to make the payments for you in the event of a disability that prevented you from working. Don't overlook this, as something like 40% of mortgage foreclosures are as a result of disability.

Some institutions offer critical illness insurance, as well. This may be valuable, but keep in mind that it is not disability coverage. You can have a critical illness without being disabled, and you can be disabled without having a critical illness that is covered by the policy.

These protections sound like a good idea and can certainly be very important in the event of death or disability. But is the automatic insurance the best way to go?

Let's keep a few things in mind.

The first thing you should know is that you are not required to take this insurance, so don't feel pressured. However, if this type of protection is valuable for you, given your circumstances and financial reserves, look seriously at some of the options.

NO BULL

Buying mortgage life insurance from your lender may protect your lender more than your family.

If the option they are offering is to add the entire cost of the policy for the term of your loan to the amount of your loan upfront, just say "no." That type of payment plan is a complete rip off. If, instead, the plan will be paid from small amounts added to your regular payments, then you can at least listen.

However, while the lender's plan might be convenient and cost-effective, a personally-owned policy may offer a number of other benefits that you will find valuable, and it may even cost less.

If you have an existing life insurance policy, you may be able to increase the amount fairly easily, without incurring a new annual policy fee. This saves a few dollars on the annual premium.

If you are over 45 but you are a "preferred risk," a personal policy might actually be cheaper than what's being offered by your mortgage lender. Insurance companies are going more and more to preferred underwriting. If you are a non-smoker, have a favourable weight-to-height ratio, low blood pressure and a family history of good health, you may be eligible for a preferred rate that decreases the premiums significantly.

Also keep in mind that the lender's insurance coverage is what's called **decreasing term**. It only covers the current outstanding balance of the loan or mortgage, which is going down all the time. However, your premium does not go down, though it is generally calculated on a normal amortization. If you make lump sum payments to pay your loan down faster, your premium will not decrease, but your amount of insurance will decrease, just as quickly as you pay your loan down.

On renewal of your loan at the end of the term, the premiums may go up by virtue of your older age. With the personal policy the same would be true, except that you can have the premium guaranteed for five, 10 or 20 years on term insurance and for life on permanent insurance.

Perhaps the most important benefit of a personal policy is its portability. This can be very attractive, and becomes critical if you lose your insurability in the future, due to a deterioration of health (or taking on dangerous hobbies). A personal life insurance policy—whether term or permanent—can never be canceled by the insurance company as long as you keep paying the premium, even if you become terminally ill.

On the other hand, such an illness would prevent you from purchasing a new policy, which you would have to do on renewal of your mortgage term.

A personally owned policy covers you even if you purchase a new house and have a new mortgage. With the lender insurance, you would need to make a new application and could have a problem if your health has changed for the worse.

The life insurance provided by the lending institutions pays the death benefits directly to the lender to discharge your loan. Your personal life insurance policy pays to the beneficiaries of your choice—usually your spouse or children. Your family can then use the proceeds to pay off the mortgage or use it for other more pressing needs.

NO BULL

A personally owned term insurance policy gives you much more flexibility than insurance tied to a loan or mortgage.

To do your homework properly, speak to one or two independent insurance brokers who can show you the alternatives and give you the prices. If the price is the same or even close, I would opt for the personal insurance. With this approach, you have an individual contract with an insurance company, rather than being part of a group plan.

This also provides a higher level of protection, flexibility and portability.

53

Disability Insurance—
What if You Can't Work?

BEING UNABLE TO WORK because of a long-term disability can have the same financial effect as death, and can even be more expensive. To be horribly crude, it can cost a lot more to care for a disabled person than to pay for funeral.

Many more people become disabled for a period of three months or longer during their careers than actually die.

Here is a shocking statistic. Currently, 14% of "work-age" Canadians are disabled, and 36% of people who become disabled remained disabled for more than one year.[13]

In the US, the Social Security Administration estimates that three in 10 workers entering the workforce today will become disabled during their careers.

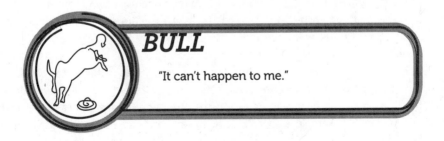

BULL

"It can't happen to me."

---

[13] Statistics Canada, Participation and Activity Limitation Survey, 2006, Catalogue no. 89-628-x. Last modified: 2009-06-22.

We always look at the financial risks to a client or the family if the client were to become disabled and unable to work, through accident or illness. In some cases, the client is able to self-insure, because adequate assets exist to provide all the necessary income, even if the breadwinner could not work.

For most of us, though, the extended disability of a breadwinner would be a serious or catastrophic financial event. In these situations, purchasing insurance is the only prudent thing to do.

Disability insurance pays a predetermined amount of monthly income after an agreed waiting period, if the policy-owner becomes totally disabled. There are many different options and definitions which make disability insurance somewhat complicated, but it is an absolute necessity for employed or self-employed people who have dependents.

The waiting period could be 30 days, 60 days or as much as one year. The longer the waiting period, the lower the premium cost for the insurance. The best way to plan out the waiting period is to calculate expenses and compare them to the cash reserves that would be available in the event of disability. Large amounts of cash reserve can fund a longer waiting period.

The benefit period could be two years, five years or to age 65. The longer the benefit period a person selects, the higher the premium. For this reason, some people bet that their disability will be temporary, and purchase one of the shorter benefit options.

The two other determinants of premium level are the age at which you start the policy—obviously, the older the more expensive—and the occupation. Insurance companies have four occupation categories, starting with one that requires significant manual labour and has a higher risk of disability, ranging to professionals who do most of their work with their brains and hands. The assumption here is that there's less chance of disability at work, and that these people would be able to return to work even if a significant portion of their bodies no longer functioned.

This last category—often referred to as 4A—offers an option called "own occupation." This is an improved definition of disability. Basic policies ("any occupation") define disability as the inability, due to accident or illness, to carry out the duties of an occupation for which the policyowner is reasonably suited based on education and experience. An "own occupation" will pay out benefits whenever the policyowner is unable to carry out the specialized duties of his or her own occupation. For example, a surgeon could have a hand injury or palsy that prevents her from performing surgery. She might be able to do an office job or another occupation, but the insurance company will continue to pay the benefits.

In this situation, these policies also allow for the person to return to work—in this example, perhaps as a general practitioner physician or medical consultant, but not as a surgeon—and the policy will pay a reduced amount to make up for the loss of income.

Some policies have a "residual disability" clause, which allows a person to return to work but have the comfort of having no waiting period for a subsequent disability, if due to the same accident or illness.

In all cases, disability benefits are tax-free if the policyowner has paid the premiums, and not deducted them as a business expense. On the other hand, if an employer pays for the insurance premiums or if the policyowner deducts them as a business expense, then the benefits received are taxable.

Most people who work for medium or large companies are covered by group disability plans. There is usually a distinction between short term disability (sometimes called income and indemnity) and long-term disability, or LTD.

Some companies, and some government employers, don't actually have the short term coverage, instead allowing employees to build up sick days that they can use during a relatively short term disability. This is dangerous, as often these sick days will be used as they become available, or to cover short-term extended illness, and are not in place when a serious accident or illness puts someone on the sidelines for a long period of time.

If you might be in that situation, fully investigate your coverage and calculate whether or not you have enough cash reserves to fund that illness, until the LTD kicks in. Most people don't have that type of funding in reserve, and therefore may require a disability policy that covers up to two years of disability.

Employment Insurance will provide some benefits to a disabled worker, if the worker suffers a 40% or higher decrease in income. The maximum benefit is about $500 per week, and all benefits are taxable.

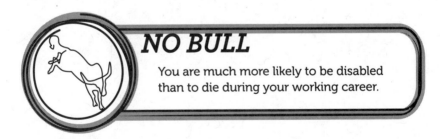

NO BULL

You are much more likely to be disabled than to die during your working career.

A waiting period applies, which only starts upon application to EI, and not when the disability begins. For those reasons, the disabled person will want to put in an application immediately. (This can be a challenge, when obviously other things would be top of mind.)

Canada Pension Plan also has a disability program, but to qualify, a person who has been contributing to CPP must suffer from a disability that is defined as "severe and prolonged." Generally, the qualification bar is higher than for the disability plans. However, if a disabled person might qualify, then it is well worth applying. If accepted, this protects a person's CPP retirement benefits, which would have been eroded while not making contributions.

The waiting period for CPP disability benefits is three months and the benefit period is to age 65.

The risk of disability is significant, and much higher than most of us would like to believe. The chance of that disability lasting long-term is also very real.

Since the inability to work would cut off your most valuable asset—your earning power—it's worth making sure that asset is properly protected, and paying for the protection you need.

54

Critical Illness Insurance is not a Replacement for Disability Insurance

CRITICAL ILLNESS INSURANCE is a relatively new (1980s) product, and it pays out an agreed sum of money if the policyowner is hit by one of a list of about 20 to 30 serious illnesses, such as cancer, heart attack, stroke, etc., whether or not the insured person is disabled by this disease.

The lump sum payment is received tax free, and could be from $25,000 to $1 million, based on how much you purchased.

Some people use the benefits to pay for out of country medical treatments, for drug or other therapies not covered by provincial medical plans, to take time off work for treatment or rehabilitation, or to pay off debts and current obligations.

For those who can afford more substantial premiums, they can also insure their future retirement savings.

These policies do not necessarily pay out if a person is disabled, and certainly don't if the disability is due to an accident or due to an illness that is not listed in the policy. For this reason, critical illness insurance is **not** a replacement for proper disability coverage that is customized to a person's situation.

Unfortunately, a number of my friends and associates have been struck by significant illnesses lately, which reminds me frequently of the potential importance and the relevance of this type of insurance.

The invention of critical illness insurance is generally attributed to South African doctor Marius Barnard, brother of heart surgeon Christiaan Barnard, who performed the first heart transplant. As Marius apparently stated by way of explanation, "People sometimes need insurance not because they are going to die, but because they are going to live."

The types of illnesses generally covered include heart attack, stroke, bypass surgery, cancer, kidney failure, blindness, deafness, organ transplants, multiple sclerosis, paralysis, severe burns, loss of limbs, loss of speech, occupational HIV injury (relevant for medical or emergency workers), and motor neuron diseases like Parkinson's and Alzheimer's.

With the incredibly high cost of drug treatments for some disorders, this type of protection can be critical, even if disability insurance is in place. According to the Canadian Cancer Society, up to 66% of the costs incurred by a cancer survivor may not be covered by any such programs.

The ability to eliminate debts and build a cash reserve can also go a long way to alleviating stress and distractions when a person should be concentrating on fighting a disease. The extra cash can also give you access to treatments in other jurisdictions, and possibly world-renowned specialists and facilities which a person could not otherwise afford.

In the absence of such coverage, or a substantial emergency fund, people are often forced to draw from their RRSP's or borrow money to fund such treatments. Since a withdrawal from an RRSP is taxable, it can take almost two dollars of RRSP to provide one dollar of net spending power.

Whether depleting RRSP's or borrowing, or simply not being able to save for a number of years, there is a serious negative effect on future retirement capital.

Each insurance company offering critical illness coverage has its own definitions and conditions for payment, which are clearly outlined in the policy contract.

Most policies have a refund of premiums option if death occurs without a claim being paid. Others allow for total refund of premium at the 10th and 20th policy anniversaries if the coverage is discontinued. This means the only cost is the investment return that could have been earned on the money.

This coverage is worth investigating, but make sure you consult an insurance representative who has become an expert in the area.

Hybrid policies

One insurance company has introduced in innovative life insurance product, which combines life, critical illness and disability insurance within a single policy. When an applicant passes the required medical underwriting criteria, the person is approved for an agreed total amount of insurance.

However, instead of this lump sum just being paid out as a death benefit or critical illness claim, the pool of money can be drawn upon to satisfy either a death claim (100% of the available pool), a critical illness claim (25% of the available pool, which then decreases the future death benefit pool) or disability insurance claim (up to 0.5% of the available pool paid per month, also decreasing the pool).

Several insurance companies have combined term insurance and critical illness, but this product, called Synergy, is the first I've seen with all three protections pooled into one. This simplifies the application process, decreases the cost of protection and may allow a lot of middle income earners to become properly protected from the varied risks they actually face.

We know we need protection, but we don't know from which danger we will end up really needing the protection. Since it's expensive to purchase each coverage separately, combining them can make a lot of sense.

55

Employer Group Health and Extended Medical Insurance

FOR MOST PEOPLE who work for companies, a portion of their life insurance needs and often all of the disability insurance needs are covered off by employer group plans. As well, such plans offer additional benefits under the umbrella of "extended health benefits," and can include:

- prescription drugs
- travel health insurance
- dental coverage
- prescription eyeglass coverage
- chiropractor and massage
- ambulance
- semi-private hospital room, if admitted to hospital
- naturopath
- psychologist and counseling services

All of these services have annual limits, and usually a "co-insurance" clause, which means the insurance company only pays part of the cost.

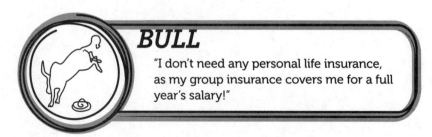

BULL

"I don't need any personal life insurance, as my group insurance covers me for a full year's salary!"

Life insurance is usually available in multiples of annual salary. For example, the basic policy might include one times annual salary, with additional multiples available as optional coverage, with an extra charge.

The basic coverage for life and disability insurance is usually provided on a non-medical basis. This means that everyone who is a member of the group is approved, and there are no health questions to complete. This is a big advantage to group insurance, for anyone with any health impairments.

Almost always, additional life insurance will require the applicant to answer medical questions. While the underwriting standards are generally a little more relaxed for group insurance plans than for individual policies (especially large ones), approval will only be granted to people in reasonable health for their age.

A good group insurance plan can be a tremendous benefit, especially for people who have regular costs for things like pharmaceuticals. The cost of these can run up very high, if a person has to pay for all of them himself. A group plan is definitely something to look for when you are shopping for employment.

Having said that, remember that one, two or even three times salary in life insurance is not nearly enough to replace a salary and look after a family for more than that number of years. Don't assume that simply belonging to a group life insurance plan has solved your life insurance needs. You will almost always need additional personal coverage to supplement that.

Travel health insurance

Whenever you leave your home province, consider purchasing travel health insurance. If you are traveling outside of Canada, then you must **absolutely** have a good quality travel insurance policy in place.

Almost all good group insurance plans include travel insurance as one of the benefits. Make sure you understand the limitations, in terms of length of trip, maximum insured value and any exclusions.

Premium credit cards also provide some travel insurance benefits if you book your trip with them, but again be very careful about exclusions.

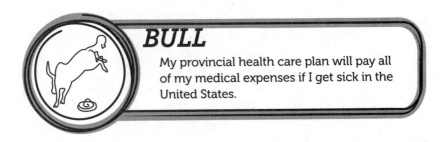

BULL

My provincial health care plan will pay all of my medical expenses if I get sick in the United States.

The reason to worry about this is that a serious illness in the United States can quickly rack up medical bills in excess of $100,000. That's not a risk you want to take. Provincial health care plans will only reimburse up to their guidelines, which may be $250-$400 per day for a stay in hospital. If you are hospitalized in an intensive care ward in the United States, the costs can run to $10,000 per day, plus extra charges for everything from cotton balls to Band-Aids to specialists.

A slip and fall in Chicago or New Orleans, with a resulting concussion and hospital stay could bankrupt a person. With the high quality of watering holes in those cities and the propensity for partying, make sure to have comprehensive travel medical coverage.

56

Avoiding Fraud and Rip-offs

Greetings,

I am Sgt. Bryan Stone, a NATO Soldier in peace keeping force in Afghanistan, I am serving in the military of the 1st Armoured Division in Afghanistan.

We managed to move some funds belonging to Al Farouq training camp in the tune of USD $45 Million Dollars in cash. We want to move this Fund out of Afghanistan to your custody and you will keep our share for us until we return to meet with you.

You are to take 30% of the total $45 Million Dollars and keep 70% for me and my colleagues. Please No strings attached, we plan on using private diplomatic courier to dispatch the Fund out of Afghanistan, if you are interested on handling this deal with me, kindly send me an email through sgtbryantone@yahoo.com.hk *indicating your interest including your confidential telephone numbers for quick communication.*

Respectfully,
Sgt. Bryan Stone

HAVE YOU RECEIVED an email like that? This is a clever and contemporary variation on the old Nigerian cash scam that has been popular for over a decade. The Sergeant Stone version is my favourite.

Now I would like to believe that you would immediately recognize this is a scam—at least when Sgt. Stone subsequently asks for your bank account information—and you would recognize that he and his friends are going to clean out your bank account, rather than make a $45 million deposit and invite you to keep almost $15 million for your trouble.

However, many current attempts to steal your money are much more subtle. These are what the information technology people call "phishing."

Every week, I receive official looking emails purporting to be from one of the major Canadian banks. The logo and return email address all look authentic. If I actually had an account with that particular bank, I would be tempted to follow their instructions.

Often, the email refers to a security problem with my account, or an improvement the bank is making in their logon procedure or something similar. They request that I go to a website and provide my account number, and sometimes my log-in ID and password.

Never, ever do this!

Your real bank will never ask you to reveal your password or other personal information. This is a phishing expedition. No legitimate financial institution contacts clients this way, and they will never ask you to reveal your account information.

My email box is also full of offers for a free credit check. These make me suspicious as, of course, such an application requires me to reveal all of my personal and banking information.

These criminals may be trying to siphon money from one of your bank accounts or, worse yet, they may be gathering enough information to steal your identity and open up new accounts and lines of credit in your name.

Your first line of defense is to be careful to never reveal your account numbers, social insurance number, passwords or any other identifying information to anyone. If you must write down your instant teller or online banking passwords, keep that well away from your bank card or computer, in case your house is broken into.

While we're on the topic of your computer, be very wary of anyone phoning or emailing you and asking you if you have a certain problem with your computer, like it's running slowly. They will purport to know how to fix it and offer to come to your home and make the necessary repairs directly on your computer. You can guess what else they're up to at the same time.

Don't accept such offers.

NO BULL

Identity theft has reached epidemic proportions, and ruined many lives.

For thorough monitoring of your identity safety, you can purchase protection through legitimate credit bureaus like Equifax or TransUnion. For $15 per month or less, they will conduct a thorough initial credit report, then monitor activity related to you and report anything suspicious. This is worth looking into, if you have reason to believe that scammers have had access to your information.

This type of theft is a real threat in the information age, and no different from people phoning you or coming door to door to "help" you with your banking, or to otherwise try to part you from your money.

Here are a few identity theft prevention tips so that you don't fall victim:

- Make sure your PIN is a number that's hard to guess (avoid using your birthday or phone number).
- Avoid sending private information, like credit card numbers, over email.
- Shred personal information when no longer needed. Don't put any identifying information into the recycling or the trash in one piece, and absolutely never dispose of bank or investment account statements without shredding them or tearing them up.
- If you shop online, make sure to shop on a secure website or look for merchants who use added security features before entering credit card information.
- Memorize your PIN so there's no need to write it down.
- Never provide your credit card number over the phone unless you initiated the call.
- Remember that your bank will never ask for personal banking information over email.

Here are some tell-tale signs that your identity has been compromised:

- Your accounts show unknown or unexplained activity.
- You don't receive your regular bills and credit card statements. Make a note of when they are due, so you are alerted to their absence. Fraudsters are not above stealing mail from your mailbox to get personal information.
- You're turned down for credit when you believe you should be in good standing. Someone may be incurring charges in your name and ruining your credit rating.
- Debt collectors contact you regarding charges that you haven't made.
- You receive credit cards in the mail that you haven't applied for.

Your wallet has been stolen—what do you do next?

- Call your credit card company immediately, and contact your bank or other financial institution and report your missing bank and credit cards. Always keep a record of the credit card company's toll-free number, separate from your wallet.
- Let your local police know in case it's turned in.

- Replace any missing ID cards, like your driver's license or birth certificate, that were in your wallet.
- If your SIN is stolen, it's important to report it to the appropriate authorities.
- You will want to monitor your credit rating, and consider purchasing a service like TransCanada or Equifax monitoring, to ensure that there's no suspicious activity.
- All of the work that's involved with replacing these items illustrates just how much time and energy it would take to restore your identity if it was compromised. Adding identity theft insurance coverage to your existing home insurance policy can give you the extra comfort of knowing that you're protected in case something like this happens.

Understanding emerging forms of identity theft like phishing or vishing
- Phishing and vishing are scams designed to trick you into providing fraudsters with your personal information.
- In phishing, the victim receives a fraudulent email that looks like it came from a legitimate company asking them to click on a link that will take them to a (fake) website. The victim is then asked to confirm their personal information, which is then captured by the fraudster.
- Vishing is a telephone version of this type of scam. Victims are usually asked to key in their personal information to fix some type of problem.

Being careful about how and where you share personal information is essential but sometimes scams still happen. If you are registered with one of the credit agencies, or have identity theft coverage included in your house policy, it's reassuring to know that you have someone on your side to help restore your identity if it's compromised.

I receive at least one of these phishing emails every single day, so there's no doubt in my mind that the phishermen are in business in a serious way.

In general, just be smart. Posting your upcoming vacation dates on Facebook is not smart. Answering emails offering you something for nothing is not smart. Telling people where you bank or invest, or giving them your access information is not smart.

Keep your private life private, and hold on to your money.

Managing the Bull:
Detect and Deflect the Crap

AS DONNA SUMMER REMINDED US in the 1970s, "You work hard for your money...," so you want to make sure you protect it and hang onto it.

Our "no bull" advice is to insure yourself against any potential losses that you can't afford to pay for yourself. This of course means guaranteeing replacement value of your house and contents, apartment contents, cars and other property, in case the worst should happen.

As I write this in July, 2012, the newspaper and radio interviews for the last two days have been filled with stories of people whose houses were flooded in the spring of 2011, even though they were 30 miles away from the river that caused the level of Lake Manitoba to rise to dangerous levels when a freak storm from the west was perfectly timed to drive all that high water right through their homes on the east side of the lake.

Why are they in the news again today?

Because 100 km/h winds and torrential rains on the weekend have once again destroyed those houses, even picking up a mobile home with two people in it and dumping it 30 meters away.

Can't happen to you? That's what I still think, as well, but I think we may both be naïve.

Avoid being the new story that everyone pities.

Part 7

Enjoying the Ride: Putting Your Plans Together

It was a beautiful day, the sun beat down
I had the radio on, I was drivin'
Trees flew by, me and Del were singin' little Runaway
I was flyin'

Yeah runnin' down a dream
That never would come to me
Workin' on a mystery, goin' wherever it leads
Runnin' down a dream

I felt so good like anything was possible
I hit cruise control and rubbed my eyes

...

There's something good waitin' down this road
I'm pickin' up whatever's mine
Runnin' down a dream

    - MICHAEL CAMPBELL, TOM PETTY, JEFF LYNNE

57

The Stages of Life

WE'VE BEEN DOING a lot of intensive work lately in helping people make firm decisions about their retirements. Each experience has reminded me of a number of fundamentals and, as always, taught me new lessons.

The best thing I've learned is a wonderful description of the stages of life. A couple of my favourite clients explained this to me. They defined these stages based on which of the following four questions people are asking you at a particular time of your life:

1. When are you going to get married?
2. When are you going to have kids?
3. When are you going to retire?

This is my clients' stage of life, and they felt like they really wanted to set a specific retirement date. Up until now, they had continually been saying "two years from now," but of course, that date kept moving.

The fourth question was said more in jest, and the clients explained, "This is the one you don't want to hear."

4. How's your health?

It's fascinating how, when you reach a certain age (which **you** don't really think is very old...) you and your friends suddenly start talking about your health as much as you do about sports or any other topic. I'm at that age, which is probably why I thought question four was so humorous.

If you're my age or older, you'll know what I'm talking about.

In a more general way, I thought those questions formed a wonderfully succinct summary of the four main stages of adult life.

When it comes to retirement, I strongly believe that more information is better than less information. The more precise you are about your projected expenses and income, the more likely you are to enter retirement with a positive sense of purpose, and with confidence.

This is the sermon I preach to my clients, when we talk about retirement.

My job is to project amounts of income, sources of income and portfolio structure that will meet the targets and avoid trouble.

NO BULL

To retire happily, you need to try and minimize surprises.

The client's responsibility (with help from us wherever we can add value), is to paint the picture of their happy retirement. This picture has to have colour, detail and depth.

What are the goals? Where will it be? What will it look like? What will it feel like? What are the activities? Who do you want to be sharing it with?

What can make it better?

This specific description can then be priced out with a surprising degree of accuracy. The projected income and projected expenses can then be matched up and compared.

Many people are afraid to put down the specifics. This may be because they suspect that they won't have enough income, but they really want to retire anyway. They simply feel that they will make up the difference somehow, or compromise on the things they want to do.

That approach usually leads to a vague, uneasy feeling, and a lack of confidence.

NO BULL

All information—whether good or bad— is important to know.

This is tragic, as it means entering retirement with a sense of fear and foreboding, when knowing the facts can usually take away that fear.

Even if it's bad news, it's better to know it. Perhaps the projected expenses exceed the projected income. Once that demon is quantified, though, it can be exorcised. Minor changes might be made to the lifestyle to make things match. Investments can be slightly more aggressive, or more efficient, to provide higher returns. Part-time work can be continued, which may be a positive addition to the lifestyle and diversity of retirement activity.

The old saying is, "Better the devil you know, than the devil you don't know." That statement is true for a lot of reasons, including the fact that, once known, that devil is never as bad in reality as your imagination made it out to be. (I'm speaking of course only of economics, not of religion or Stephen King novels. Or am I?)

At a meeting with clients this past week, my theory was reinforced, when my clients said they wanted to follow the advice they got from a retired woman at their lake. The woman said to them, "A year before we retired, I wished someone had sat us down and made us determine exactly what our expenses were going to be after we quit. There have been a lot of surprises and a few shocks, and this could have been avoided, if we just sat down and thought it through."

As usual, someone said it better than I could.

58

Generating Income for Living

ONE OF THE MOST IMPORTANT THINGS we do as financial planners is help people properly structure their affairs to produce their required retirement income, on a safe and tax-effective basis.

You will hopefully be retired for at least 20 to 30 years. Think back 30 years to food and gas prices, interest rates, market levels and the demographics of the Canadian population, for an idea of how much everything can change during that period. Virtually everyone agrees that the pace of change is increasing.

Thorough and proper planning involves a lot more than simply setting up a systematic withdrawal plan on a balanced mutual fund, as some advisors would suggest. Since most advisors have spent their careers helping people accumulate money for retirement, there has traditionally been a lack of training and experience in designing income plans. Luckily, this is changing.

To give you a vivid example of why this is so important, let's look at someone who retired at the end of 1962, and withdrew a constant 7% from their portfolio, which was invested in a balanced portfolio of 60% stocks and 40% bonds.

Thirty years later, that person had run out of money.

However, if that same person had retired at the end of 1963 with the same amount of money—just one year later—they would still have almost all their capital left 30 years later.

This brings us to concept number one—luck. The most comprehensive and sophisticated analysis of data from the last 150 years concluded that the number one determinant of financial success in retirement is luck, and more specifically, the timing of the retirement.

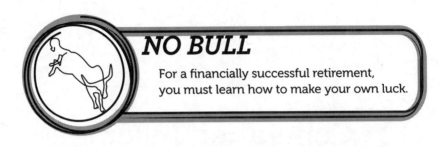

NO BULL

For a financially successful retirement,
you must learn how to make your own luck.

If the market goes down for the first two years of retirement, and the retiree continues to draw on investments that have declined, it is very difficult to recover. On the other hand, if a person retires at the bottom of the market cycle and has a few good years to start, they put "money in the bank" that will likely see them through.

Proper retirement planning is about eliminating the effects of luck and the potential ill effects of bad timing. It's also about measuring progress regularly throughout retirement, and making adjustments as necessary.

Here are **Dave's Five Rules for Retirement Income Planning**:

1. Never sell low;
2. Use investments which generate regular, dependable income, hopefully adequate for your needs;
3. Avoid "Systematic Withdrawal Plans" and any other automatic selling mechanism when applied to fluctuating investments;
4. Determine your *Sustainable Withdrawal Rate* and plan within it;
5. Consider annuities for a base of income, if you crave security.

That all sounds simple, but it's challenging to properly structure and execute. Consideration must be given to tax brackets, income-tested tax credits and government benefits, use of the pension transfer provisions, when to withdraw from RRSPs and, above all, your personal vision for your retirement and, ultimately, your estate.

Here are several potential sources of your income in retirement, and the general order in which to draw them:

1. Government benefits, primarily Canada Pension Plan and Old Age Security (fully taxable);
2. Company pension, if any (fully taxable);
3. Income distributions paid by investments (fully taxable if interest; reduced rate for dividends);
4. Capital withdrawals from investments (tax-free);
5. Capital gains (half taxable);
6. RRSP and RRIF income (fully taxable).

One question to always remember is, "Where is the most efficient place from which to take my next $100 of income, taking everything into consideration?"

The answer will be more complex than you expect, so it usually pays to get some outside advice. Your financial planner, investment advisor and accountant all have a role to play.

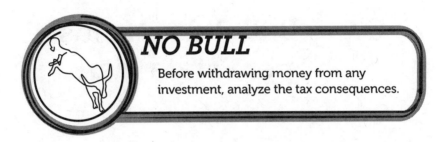

NO BULL

Before withdrawing money from any investment, analyze the tax consequences.

If you are heading toward retirement—or enjoying the wonderful time of life now—here are three books you should consider reading:

1. *Your Retirement Income Blueprint* by Daryl Diamond[16];
2. *Master Your Retirement* (2012 Edition) by Douglas V. Nelson[17]; and
3. *Retirement's Harsh New Realities* by Gordon Pape.[18]

We want this to be the best time of your life, so head into it fully prepared!

16 Diamond, Darryl; *Your Retirement Income Blueprint—A Six-Step Plan to Design and Build a Secure Retirement*; John Wiley & Sons Canada, Ltd. 2011.
17 Nelson, Douglas V., *Master Your Retirement—How to fulfill your dreams with peace of mind*; The Knowledge Bureau, 2012.
18 Pape, Gordon; *Retirement's Harsh New Realities—Protecting Your Money in a Changing World*; Penguin Canada, 2012.

59

Every Bull Rider Needs a Proper Estate Plan

STOP ME IF YOU'VE HEARD THIS BEFORE—you need to have a Will and Power of Attorney.

Having a signed, valid, accurate, up-to-date Will is going to save your family a ton of hassle when you die, will reduce legal and other fees associated with death, may save taxes, and will ensure that your estate goes to the people you want to receive it.

Without a valid Will, there is no guarantee your wishes will be carried out at all. The only guarantee is a more complicated estate settlement process, with all of the delays, costs and animosity that come with that unpleasant experience.

Your provincial government rules will actually determine who gets your estate. How well does that idea sit with you?

Remarkably, various studies show that as many as 50% of adult Canadians don't have a current Will. Maybe they intend to live forever; maybe they're afraid that somehow signing a Will is going to hasten their demise. Neither belief is true. Methinks that in many cases it's simply procrastination, often born of a lack of knowledge or information.

Bad news, folks—you will, one day, depart this mortal coil, whether or not you then go on to live forever in the paradise or punishment of your choice. So make it possible for family and friends to mourn you without layering on the extra burden of trying to settle an estate without a proper Will.

Do it now, because you may not be able to do it in the future.

The law says that you must understand what you are doing—in technical terms, have legal capacity—in order to make a Will, draw up a Power of Attorney, sign a contract or continue to manage your own financial and business affairs. That capacity can easily be lost through injury, illness, dementia or aging. Some of these conditions are reversible; many are permanent.

If, when you lose legal capacity, you do not have a valid Power of Attorney document in place which names another individual as your "attorney," then you might end up with no control over how your affairs are handled.

In the absence of a named attorney who can take on the job, someone will have to apply to the Court to be named as your "committee." In terms of pronunciation and legal effect, this is not like the social committee, but rather closer to "the person who commits you." If there is no one willing and able to take on these tasks (or acceptable to the Court), then your affairs may be turned over to the Public Trustee in your province.

There are several drawbacks to any of these outcomes. First, any Court process is costly, especially if it has to involve lawyers, which is usually the case. Secondly, the person with the most motivation to be your committee is often the one who ends up with the job, and this is not necessarily the person you would have chosen and named, if you had gotten around to it.

Enduring Powers of Attorney are powerful documents that allow you to appoint someone to help manage your financial affairs in the event that you are unable to do so yourself. The person doing that job using such a document is known as the "attorney," which in this context does not mean "lawyer."

There are many circumstances where the Power of Attorney might be used, ranging from the attorney helping out with banking or other tasks while you maintain control of your financial affairs, to the attorney having to take complete control as a result of mental incompetence.

NO BULL
The need for a proper Power of Attorney can range from convenient to critical without warning.

But let's assume the right person gets the job, and it only costs a few thousand dollars in extra expenses. Being a committee rather than a named attorney is still inferior, as the powers may be more limited than you could have granted under your Power of Attorney. This restricts the person's ability to act on your behalf.

Finally, the person acting as committee is generally required to pass accounts (give a full accounting of actions) before the court each year.

You definitely want your Power of Attorney instrument to be "enduring." This means that it will survive your incapacity or infirmity.

A basic Power of Attorney names one or more persons, or a trust company, and gives them the legal authority to conduct business in your place and instead, within the limits set in the document. These limits can be narrow, or very broad and comprehensive.

A more sophisticated Power of Attorney can specify things like having the attorney continue your previous pattern of donations and continuing support for one or more family members.

Guaranteed care

You can also list details on the type of care you want and how much—if any—of your investment capital you want used to look after you, versus being preserved for your family or beneficiaries through your estate.

You can see the advantage to specifying this. In the absence of such direction, a benevolent family member or committee may be in the dark and left guessing as to your preferences. How many times have you heard people say, "Dad would have wanted us to spend this money on him, not keep it for us, so let's buy that thing for him now." Perhaps more often is heard the statement, "Mom wouldn't want us to spend so much money on her; she would want to add it to our future inheritance...)

A malevolent attorney or committee can be stingy with your money, hoarding it for future generations, while significantly compromising your care in the meantime. If you lack legal capacity, then you don't have the legal authority to do anything about it.

A power-of-attorney can be **subsisting**, which means it is valid and in force as soon as you sign it. Alternatively, the document can be "**springing**," which means it only becomes effective when a certain event occurs, like medical certification of the fact that you no longer have the legal capacity to enter into a contract or conduct your own affairs.

If you are uncomfortable naming one person, you can name two or more jointly, who must act in concert. Think carefully about whether this will provide protection, or instead inaction and chaos. If there is no one who stands out in your mind as the right person, then a trust company is a consideration.

The main message is to take care of this now. It is too late once you or a loved one has suffered a health setback or accident which renders you unable to conduct your own affairs.

This is particularly important since it is estimated that 5.5 million Canadians will be affected by dementia between 2008 and 2038.

You may also want to prepare a document empowering someone to make health care decisions for you, if you are unable. They have different names in different provinces, like Power of Attorney for Health, Advanced Health Care Directive or Living Will. In these, you name a person you trust as your healthcare proxy and specify the limits you want set on extraordinary measures taken to keep you alive.

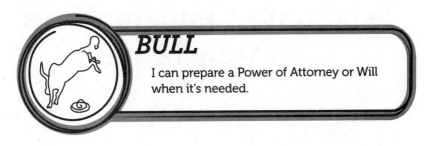

BULL

I can prepare a Power of Attorney or Will when it's needed.

60

Giving Back: Becoming a Philanthropist on Your Terms

AT SOME POINT you will realize that you have achieved a lot of success in your life, if you really let yourself acknowledge that fact without false modesty.

Your achievements are likely many, and you have overcome obstacles and challenges. Take a minute to think about those things, and let yourself enjoy the feeling that brings.

Now, does that start leading you to thoughts about your legacy and the permanent things you will leave behind? I guess what I am suggesting here is appreciating your own success, and letting yourself evolve that into thinking about "significance."

Many philanthropic organizations have an arrangement where you can leave them money after you are gone. For most of us, that's the time we will be able to make a gift of greater significance.

Can I suggest you think about the organizations that have made a difference to you in your life, or the ones you think can make the most significant improvement to your community in the future?

Making a bequest in your Will is the most common gifting method. You simply put a clause in your Will that says that a certain percentage of the residue of your estate (or a predetermined lump sum) will be left from your estate to one or more philanthropic organizations. This can also be a conditional gift, for instance only taking place if a primary beneficiary has passed away before you do, or unconditional.

Your executors will write the cheque or, if you have stocks, flow-through shares, real estate, art or other capital property that has appreciated in value, they will make the donation "in-kind," which means your estate will be exempt from capital gain on the disposition of that particular asset.

In that situation, the 44% combined federal and provincial tax credit, and the elimination of tax on the capital gain that would otherwise be payable, could mean that your estate ends up with more after-tax money after making the gift. (In most cases, there is a cost to the estate, but the maximum is about 56% of the gift, after the tax credit.)

Some people who are charitably inclined will purchase a life insurance policy, and name charities as beneficiaries. This creates additional estate value and a larger tax credit usable against other taxes on death, on things like capital gains and the collapse of RRIFs.

Alternatively, the charities can be named as *contingent* beneficiary, which means they only receive the money if your first choice is already dead when you die.

For immediate tax benefits, the ownership of a life insurance policy can be transferred to a charitable organization and a tax credit will be granted today for the cash value of the policy.

You will also get a tax credit for any premiums you continue to pay.

Another method of gifting on death is to name a charitable organization as the beneficiary of your RRSP or RRIF. You can designate all, or some, of your different plans. Since the collapse of these will be taxable on death, leaving some of it to a charity to create a tax credit to offset some of that tax liability may make a lot of sense.

Don't do this if you're married, because passing the RRSP or RRIF to a spouse on death defers the tax until the second death. Therefore, naming a charity as the contingent (or second choice) beneficiary—after your spouse—is often a plan to consider.

Above all, get some good professional advice before you set such plans in motion.

Often, creative planning can allow you to leave a substantial gift to a charity, without a significant reduction to the amount you leave to your family.

My best advice is to put your affairs in order, no matter what your current age, so that your wishes are carried out and taxes, probate and legal fees minimized.

Buy enough life insurance so that your family will survive (or have a chance to thrive) after you are gone.

Take care of things so that your loved ones can have the time they need to properly grieve. That's a very real, inevitable human need when faced with a loss. The greater and closer the loss, the greater the need.

NO BULL

Prepare a proper estate plan NOW, as no one knows when they'll get bucked off.

Give them also the opportunity to celebrate a life well-lived, and to join with others in appreciating the impact you had on their lives, the things that made you special and unforgettable, and the things they will miss the most.

Make yours a life to celebrate. Never go to bed angry at your spouse or family. Think about what you would miss about someone if they were gone, and tell them now what you appreciate about them.

And think about all the things for which you feel grateful. I guarantee that process will feel wonderful.

Managing the Bull:
Detect and Deflect the Crap

WE'VE COME A LONG WAY, you and I. We started at the beginning, which is deciding where **you** want to go, making your vision real and committing to it. Go back now and review your mission statement, and recommit to it.

Thank you for letting me be your companion in preparation for your life journey. I am truly honoured and humbled by the opportunity to help.

I sincerely hope that many parts of *Managing the Bull* will help you become clearer on the things that are most important to you, add to your repertoire of tools and techniques to reach your goals, and ultimately help you to build the life you really want.

Remember, don't sweat the small stuff, and try to decide that, ultimately, it's all small stuff.

Side-step the crap, be grateful for everything you have and enjoy every minute. ***All the best!***

Appendix 1

Selected Financial and Investment Organizations

- **Advocis—the Financial Advisors Association of Canada** www.advocis.ca, tel: 1-800-563-5822, info@advocis.ca

  Advocis is the trade organization of life insurance and mutual fund advisors, primarily. It was formed by a merger between the Canadian Association of Insurance and Financial Advisors (CAIFA) and the Canadian Association of Financial Planners (CAFP).

  Industry recognized designations: Certified Financial Planner (CFP), Chartered Life Underwriter (CLU) and Certified Health Insurance Specialist (CHS).

- **CFA Institute**, www.cfasociety.org, tel: 1-800-247-8132

  The CFA Institute grants and administers the CFA Charter, and sets standards for consistency in performance of investment portfolios. The Chartered Financial Analyst (CFA®) Program is a globally recognized standard for measuring the competence and integrity of financial analysts.

- **Financial Planning Standards Council,** www.fpsccanada.org, tel: 1-800-305-9886, inform@fpsc.ca

  Financial Planning Standards Council (FPSC®), develops, promotes and enforces professional standards in financial planning through Certified Financial Planner® certification, and raises Canadians› awareness of the importance of financial planning. FPSCs vision is to see Canadians improve their lives by engaging in financial planning.

  Industry recognized designation: Certified Financial Planner (CFP®)

- **Institute of Advanced Financial Planners** www.IAFP.ca, tel: 1-888-298-3292, information@iafp.ca

  This is the professional organization of the most qualified financial planners, those who hold the R.F.P.® (Registered Financial Planner) professional designation. R.F.P.s must show both proficiency and experience in comprehensive financial planning, in order to achieve and maintain the designation, as well as annually sign a pledge to the Code of Professional Ethics, and prove 30 hours of ongoing professional development.

  Industry recognized designation: Registered Financial Planner (R.F.P.®)

- **Investor Education Fund**, www.investorED.ca, contactus@getsmarteraboutmoney.ca

  Investor Education Fund (IEF) develops and promotes independent financial information, programs and tools to help consumers make better financial and investing decisions. It was established as a non-profit organization by the Ontario Securities Commission and is funded by settlements and fines from OSC enforcement proceedings.

- **Investment Industry Association of Canada**, www.iiac.ca, tel: 1-416-364-2754, info@iiac.ca

  IIAC is a member-based professional association with 180 investment dealer members representing a majority of IIROC registered organizations (see below).

- **Investment Industry Regulatory Organization of Canada**, www.iiroc.ca, tel: 1-877-442-4322, InvestorInquiries@iiroc.ca

  IIROC is the SRO (self-regulatory organization) for investment dealers and investment advisors, which has regulatory responsibilities for setting and enforcing rules on the proficiency, business and financial conduct of dealer firms and their registered employees. It also sets and enforces market integrity rules regarding trading activity on Canadian equity marketplaces.

- **Knowledge Bureau**, www.knowledgebureau.com, tel: 1-866-953-4769, reception@knowledgebureau.com

  Knowledge Bureau provides continuing professional development and staff training to accountants, bookkeepers, tax practitioners, investment and financial advisors, leading to certification and designation. Courses from Knowledge Bureau are endorsed by accrediting bodies in tax and financial services. Designates specialize in managing clients' wealth as part of an inter-advisory team.

  Industry recognized designations: Master Financial Advisor (MFA™) and Distinguished Financial Advisor (DFA-Tax Services Specialist™)

- **The Ontario Securities Commission**, www.osc.gov.on.ca, tel: 1-877-785-1555, inquiries@osc.gov.on.ca.

  The Ontario Securities Commission administers and enforces securities law in the province of Ontario, with significant influence across the country. Each province has an equivalent Commission, with mandates to provide protection to investors from unfair, improper and fraudulent practices, and foster fair and efficient capital markets and confidence in capital markets.

- **Canadian Securities Administrators**, www.securities-administrators.ca, tel: 1-514-864-9510, csa-acvm-secretariat@acvm-csa.ca

  Securities regulators from each of the 10 provinces and three territories in Canada formed the CSA, to coordinate their regulations, and assist in carrying out the mandates of the Securities Commissions.

- **Society of Trust and Estate Practitioners**, www.step.ca, tel: 1-877-991-4949, stepcanada@step.ca

  STEP Canada was founded in 1998, with about 2,000 members with branches in Atlantic Canada, Montréal, Ottawa, Toronto, Winnipeg, Calgary, Edmonton and Vancouver.

  STEP is a multi-disciplinary organization with the most experienced and senior practitioners in the field, including: lawyers, accountants, financial planners, insurance advisors and trust professionals. They provide domestic and international advice on trusts and estates, including planning, administration and related taxes.

  Industry recognized designations: Trust and Estate Practitioner (TEP)

Appendix 2

Great Reads

Bach, David (2007). *Start Late, Finish Rich—A No-Fail Plan for Achieving Financial Freedom at Any Age*. Toronto, Canada. Double Day Canada.

Chilton, David (2011). *The Wealthy Barber Returns*. Kitchener, Ontario. Financial Awareness Corp.

Diamond, Darryl (2011). *Your Retirement Income Blueprint—A Six-Step Plan to Design and Build a Secure Retirement*. John Wiley & Sons Canada, Ltd.

Foran, Pat (2011). *The Smart, Savvy Young Consumer—How to save and spend wisely*. Winnipeg, Manitoba. Knowledge Bureau Newsbooks.

Jacks, Evelyn (2012). *Essential Tax Facts 2013 Edition—Secrets and Strategies for Take-Charge People*. Winnipeg, Manitoba. Knowledge Bureau NewsBooks.

Jacks, Evelyn (2012). *Jacks on Tax—Your Do-It-Yourself Guide to Filing Taxes Online*. Winnipeg, Manitoba. Knowledge Bureau Newsbooks.

Kinder, George. (1999), *The Seven Stages of Money Maturity—Understanding the Spirit and Value of Money in Your Life*. New York. Random House.

Lennick, Doug (2010). *Financial Intelligence—How to Make Smart, Values-Based Decisions with your Money and Your Life*. Denver, Colorado. FPA Press.

Nelson, Douglas. V. (2012). *Master Your Retirement—How to fulfill your dreams with peace of mind*. Winnipeg, Manitoba. Knowledge Bureau NewsBooks.

Pape, Gordon (2012). *Retirement's Harsh New Realities—Protecting Your Money in a Changing World*. Toronto, Ontario. Penguin Group (Canada).

Ruta, Jim (2009). *Master Your Money Management—How to manage the advisors who work for you*. Winnipeg, Manitoba. Knowledge Bureau Newsbooks.

Index